CON

MW01016336

CONCILIUM

ADVISORY COMMITTEE

Gregory Baum	Montreal/QC. Canada
José Oscar Beozzo	São Paulo, SP Brazil
Wim Beuken	Louvain, Belgium
Leonardo Boff	Petrópolis, Brazil
John Coleman	Los Angeles, CA. USA
Norbert Greinacher	Tübingen, Germany
Gustavo Gutiérrez	Lima, Peru
Hermann Häring	Tübingen, Germany
Werner G. Jeanrond	Oslo, Norway
Jean-Pierre Jossua	Paris, France
Maureen Junker-Kenny	Dublin, Ireland
François Kabasele Lumbala	Kinshasa, Rep. Dem. Congo
Nicholas Lash	Cambridge, UK
Mary-John Mananzan	Manila, The Philippines
Alberto Melloni	Reggio, Emilia Italy
Norbert Mette	Münster, Germany
Dietmar Mieth	Tübingen, Germany
Jürgen Moltmann	Tübingen, Germany
Teresa Okure	Port Harcourt, Nigeria
Aloysius Pieris	Kelaniya/Colombo, Sri Lanka
Giuseppe Ruggieri	Catania, Italy
Paul Schotsmans	Louvain ,Belgium
Janet Martin Soskice	Cambridge, UK
Elsa Tamez	San José, Costa Rica
Christoph Theobald	Paris, France
David Tracy	Chicago, Ill. USA
Marciano Vidal	Madrid, Spain
Ellen van Wolde	Tilburg, The Netherlands
Johannes Zizioulas	Pergamo, Turkey
Regina Ammicht Quinn	Tübingen Germany
Hille Haker	Chicago, USA
Jon Sobrino	San Salvador, El Salvador
Luiz Carlos Susin	Porto Alegre, Brazil
Silvia Scatena	Bologna, Italy
Susan A. Ross	USA, Los Angeles
Solange Lefebvre	Montreal/QC. Canada
Erik Borgman	Amsterdam, Netherlands
Andres Torres Queiruga	Santiago, Spain

CONCILIUM 2020/2

Masculinities:
Theological and Religious Challenges

Edited by

Susan Abraham,
Geraldo De Mori and Stefanie Knauss

Published in 2020 by SCM Press, 3rd Floor, Invicta House, 108–114 Golden Lane, London EC1Y 0TG.

SCM Press is an imprint of Hymns Ancient & Modern Ltd (a registered charity) 13A Hellesdon Park Road, Norwich NR6 5DR, UK

Copyright © International Association of Conciliar Theology, Madras (India)

www.concilium.in

English translations copyright © 2020 Hymns Ancient & Modern Ltd.

All rights reserved. No part of this publication may be reproduced, stored in a retrieval system, or transmitted, in any form or by any means, electronic, mechanical, photocopying or otherwise, without the prior written permission of the Board of Directors of Concilium.

ISBN 978-0-334-05957-8

Printed in the UK by
Ashford, Hampshire

Concilium is published in March, June, August, October, December

Contents

Editorial

In the political moment of today, it is important to reflect on masculinities, drawing on the particular resources of theology: strongmen dominate the political stage in a number of countries, East, West and South; the #MeToo and #ChurchToo movements have given voice to the silenced victims of sexual abuse, perpetrated primarily by men; industrial and financial corporations are, to an overwhelming degree, managed by men who thus control financial, environmental and social resources. Traditional gender roles still shape men's lives to a considerable degree: about a third of young fathers take paternal leave where it is possible, but the rate has remained equal or even dropped in recent years, and overall, men still spend less time with care work or chores.[1] And yet we also begin to see a wider range of socially accepted expressions of masculinity. For individuals negotiating their gendered subjectivity, the self-centred aggressive alpha-male is an available model just as the emotionally integrated man, the straight guy who is after uncomplicated hook-ups as well as the gay man who lives in a monogamous relationship, as well as every other combination of traits that are a part of an individual's performance of gender. Ezra Chitando's article on sexualities and masculinities in the African context exemplifies this plurality of formative discourses, in his case African traditions, Christianity and Islam. In addition, while western notions of masculinity dominate the imaginary on a global scale, they are, of course, not the only models available regionally or locally,[2] as Angélica Otazú shows in her analysis of the gender system of the Guarani, an indigenous people in the Río de la Plata region.

This picture shows that discourses about masculinity are multiple and contradictory, and even an idealized image of 'hegemonic masculinity' (Raewyn Connell) is hard to define unambiguously in a given social context – hence the plural 'masculinities' in this issue's title. In addition, each hegemonic ideal of masculinity also contains internal incoherences and contradictions: the gun-toting he-male might seem like the ultimate expression of masculine supremacy, yet as Connell argues in this volume, if a man needs a gun to defend his position of masculine power, he does not actually have legitimacy.

Masculinity studies show that reference to an easy binary of men and women is not helpful, even if often difficult to escape: even supposedly less toxic ideals of masculinity can ultimately reinforce problematic essentialist stereotypes shaped by patriarchal hierarchies if, say, emotionality remains identified with femininity even if integrated into masculine identity, rendering a man more feminine (or even 'effeminate') rather than simply being taken as one of the many elements that can make up a version of masculinity. The continued struggle against the easy assumptions of binary essentialism is visible also in the contributions in this volume, even if the authors agree on the formative impact of social discourses on masculinities.

The critical study of masculinities thus has to take into account that notions of gender circulate and interrelate in complex arrangements of power and larger social systems of domination (patriarchy, white supremacy, colonialism, heteronormativity and others). This affects individuals who experience their masculine identity in terms of power or powerlessness amidst these 'interlocking systems of domination', as Vincent Lloyd writes in his analysis of the autobiography of Black gang leader Stanley Tookie Williams in which he traces his struggles over masculinity and fatherhood in a racist system. But it also shapes social and political dynamics: writing from the situation of postcoloniality, Shyam Pakhare discusses the way in which notions of 'muscular masculinity', personified in the western Christian colonizer, sustained colonial power in India, and the role that Gandhi's recourse to alternative models of masculinity based in Hinduism played in Indian independence. In a more contemporary setting, Nicholas Denysenko traces the ways in which religious discourses of masculine superiority and feminine (or feminized masculine) subordination are interwoven with the politics of the Putin government to legitimate and stabilize Russian imperialism.

What contribution can religious and theological analysis then make in this situation? How can a theological perspective on historical and contemporary constructions of masculinities contribute to creating relationships on the micro- and macro-level that allow individuals to flourish in a context of equality and justice? Can Galatians 3.28 be a guide as we negotiate theologically the discourses of masculinities in our societies, with its vision of ultimate unity in the body of Christ, when social distinctions of gender, ethnicity and status no longer play a role? Or does it simply render invisible – and thus reinforces – existing social inequality? In his foundational contribution, Herbert Anderson proposes a broad theological framework to challenge toxic masculinity in the patriarchal system, a framework that includes both changes in the structure of the church, our language about God, the need to appreciate multiplicity and interdependence and to accept vulnerability and humility.

As the contributions in this volume show, theology is called to engage ideals of masculinity with an (at least) two-fold intention: on the one hand, the self-critical reflection on the ways in which Christianity has supported the creation and reinforcement of notions of masculinity that uphold hierarchical structures from which (some) men benefit at the expense of subordinate 'others', both men and women. On the other hand, theologies can contribute creative resources for imagining ways of performing masculinities that foster equality, visions of hope and healing for individuals and groups. The question of power comes then to the fore, again, both with regard to the implication of religion in political power relationships (as Denysenko shows) and with regard to the specific situation of the Catholic Church in which a particular form of masculinity has formed to stabilize power relations within the Church. Theresia Heimerl situates clerical masculinity – which over time has become characterized primarily by abstention from the practice of heterosexuality – in its historical and theological context, whereas Julie Rubio and Leonardo Boff focus on the intersection between masculinity, sexuality and power in the current sexual abuse crisis in the Church. While Boff proposes, on the background of his psychosexual analysis, the abolishment of celibacy as a way to heal the deformations of clerical masculinity, Heimerl and Rubio suggest that broader transformations both on the structural and theoretical level are needed.

The subversive possibilities of Christianity are highlighted in Manuel Villalobos Mendoza's contribution: his analysis of the masculinity of the young man in Mark who witnesses Jesus' arrest shows that the young man is depicted as not living up to Greco-Roman masculinity, and yet he is accepted as a part of Jesus' movement, thus challenging and subverting the hegemonic ideals of Mark's context – and maybe in our times, as well. Otazú's discussion of Guarani masculinity and religion also provides alternative ways of imagining masculinity in terms of interconnectedness, with others and the cosmos. Lloyd, Anderson and Connell point towards the resources available in religious traditions for the development of plural masculinities that can in their own way contribute to the flourishing of the individual and social relationships rather than upholding systems of domination.

Yet, as the contributions in this issue show, for this to be achieved, social systems and their expectations on individual gender performance need to change alongside changes on the individual level. Theological reflections, as offered here, can provide both critical and creative resources to do so.

The Forum of this issue includes a brief report by Felipe Maia on the Pan-Amazon Synod held in Rome in October 2019, addressing some of its main issues in the context of the opposition the synod has faced by Brazilian 'strongman', President Bolsanaro. The second contribution by Benoît Vermander illustrates the situation of the Catholic Church in China and some of the fears and opportunities that the recent accord signed by the Chinese government and the Vatican might create.

Susan Abraham, Geraldo De Mori and Stefanie Knauss

Notes

1. Javier Cerrato and Eva Cifre, 'Gender Inequality in Household Chores and Work-Family Conflict', *Frontiers in Psychology* 9.1330 (2018), doi:10.3389/fpsyg.2018.01330; for parental leave policies and data in the US, see United States Department of Labour, 'Paternity Leave: Why Parental Leave for Fathers Is So Important for Working Families', https://www.dol.gov/sites/dolgov/files/OASP/legacy/files/PaternityBrief.pdf.
2. See Raewyn Connell and James W. Messerschmidt, 'Hegemonic Masculinity: Rethinking the Concept', *Gender and Society*, 19.6 (2005), 829–859.

Part One: Masculinity Studies: Current Questions, New Directions

Men, Masculinity, God:
Can Social Science Help with the
Theological Problem?

RAEWYN CONNELL

This paper introduces research on men and masculinities. Old questions took a new form in the wake of the women's liberation and gay liberation movements. A world-wide field of social-science research has developed, rapidly finding practical applications. Conceptual debates emerged, especially around the concept of hegemonic masculinity. Studies in the postcolonial world are increasingly important and point to plurality and instability in gender orders. We need to relate these to the contradictions over privilege and exclusion in religious traditions.

I Introduction

In a piece written late in life, the Irish poet W.B. Yeats had his imaginary hermit-philosopher Ribh denouncing St Patrick in these words:

> "An abstract Greek absurdity has crazed the man –
> Recall that masculine Trinity."[1]

Ribh demands a story of passion involving 'man, woman, child' – for a hermit, he's wonderfully heteronormative! – but he has put his finger on a sore point. Where are the women in this theology? Why is Godhead only masculine? And what does it mean to represent God as masculine, anyway?

In severely practical terms, most religious institutions prioritize men. The Catholic church simply excludes women from the priesthood, and therefore from becoming bishops or popes. Most Protestant churches excluded women from the ministry until quite recently, and there is still much resistance to change.

In all major divisions of Islam, the clerics or religious scholars (*ulama*) are men. Though some Islamic feminist groups do exist, the globally ascendant Salafi current of Sunni Islam, financed by the oil wealth of the Saudis, is notably male-supremacist. Even Buddhism as an organized practice is dominated by men. Some of its classic texts are simply abusive of women.

So the marginalization of women is not an accident. The ceremonial and organizational practices that prioritize men are widely legitimated by blurring religious authority with masculinity.

It's worthwhile, then, to consider what research on men and masculinity tells us, that might be useful in rethinking religion and its gender politics.

II Emergence of a research field

If you go to the Google Scholar database and look up 'masculinities', you will find about 180,000 entries. It is not a gigantic field in comparison with a topic like 'climate change', but it is a significant area of knowledge with a rich research base.

This became recognized as a field of research in the English-speaking world in the 1980s, though its roots are much earlier.[2] Debates about gender, including fears about masculinity, bubbled up in Europe and in the colonized world in the 19th and early 20th centuries, especially as women's movements took shape. The Boy Scout movement was one product of these anxieties. Arguably fascism was another.

Gender and sexuality were strongly emphasised in psychoanalysis, whose influence grew in the first half of the 20th century. By the mid-century, questions about men's social position and the state of masculinity were being raised in many forums. There was angst in the United States about the weakening of boys' moral fibre caused by (depending on who was speaking) over-protective mothers, comic books, homosexuality, or communism. At this time too the poet and cultural theorist Octavio Paz problematized 'machismo'. In a famous essay on Mexican society and culture, *The Labyrinth of Solitude*, Paz explored the stark gender divide in urban culture and the rigidity of the accepted form of masculinity. The

Labyrinth triggered a long discussion of machismo in Latin American societies.[3]

These discussions took a new shape in the 1970s. Both Women's Liberation and Gay Liberation gave an impulse towards a *social* critique of masculinity. As activist movements, they centred their gaze on questions of power and oppression. In the 1980s a research field crystallized, influenced by these questions. Researchers undertook new empirical studies and offered new ideas about gender hierarchy. Crucially, the early research showed that there is not just one pattern of masculinity.

A notable example was *Der Mann*, the book published in 1985 by two feminist researchers, Sigrid Metz-Göckel and Ursula Müller.[4] This was based on a comprehensive survey of the situation of men in Germany and their outlook on gender issues, one of the first such studies anywhere. The researchers found much complacency about everyday inequalities in family life, housework and child care. But they also found a wide spectrum of attitudes on gender equality among men, from male-chauvinism to egalitarianism. The same year a team of Australian researchers, of whom I was one, published our proposal for 'a new sociology of masculinity', emphasizing the multiplicity of masculinities and the power differences between groups of men.

A wave of social-science research followed, using surveys, close-focus interviews, content analysis and participant observation. Its main concern was to document the patterns of masculinity found in social life in particular times and places. There were studies of schools, workplaces, communities, media, and more. I call this the 'ethnographic moment' in masculinity research.

This research quickly found practical applications. Work on boys' education was given urgency by a media panic about boys' supposed failure in schooling. Programs for violence prevention, including domestic violence, drew guidance from the new masculinity research. In men's health work, the research corrected the simple dichotomous view of gender that had been taken for granted (and regrettably still persists) in biomedical sciences.

Psychological counselling, conflict resolution, criminology and sports were other areas where masculinities research proved useful. In 2003, United Nations agencies sponsored a discussion of policies concerning men, boys and masculinities, which drew on 'ethnographic moment' research around the world. This resulted in a wide-ranging document *The Role of Men and Boys in Achieving Gender Equality*, adopted at the 2004 meeting of the UN Commission on the Status of Women.[5]

The new research field grew rapidly on a world scale. The most sustained research and documentation program was launched in the mid 1990s, not in the global North, but in Chile under the leadership of Teresa Valdés and José Olavarría.[6] This program attracted researchers from across Latin America, and has produced a long series of books and reports. In 2018, a conference held in Santiago celebrated the twentieth anniversary of the first continent-wide gathering of Latin American researchers in the field.

We now have bodies of masculinity research not only from the Americas but also from Scandinavia, central Europe, Africa, the Arabic-speaking world, Australia, east Asia, Indonesia, and more. There are dedicated journals, handbooks, textbooks, university courses and conferences – all the familiar machinery of an active research field.

III Concepts

Masculinity research has seen active debates about concepts and methods. In everyday speech we often measure informally, speaking of a very masculine or a less masculine man (or woman). Some people think that to make a concept scientific, it must be quantified. In the United States particularly, a number of 'scales' of masculinity have been devised. Statistical analysis has identified as many as eleven factors within these measures – it is not a simple field!

Another debate concerns the concept of masculinity itself. If our concern is basically with men, do we need a concept of masculinity at all? Some doubt it. But if our concern is basically with gender practices and the structures of inequality that they produce, then we do need a concept of masculinities. Another debate concerns the significance of the post-structuralist turn in social science and the humanities, which emphasises the discursive construction of identities. Some scholars see this as a decisive issue for studies of masculinity. Others see it as an addition to the tool kit but less important than postcolonial and practical issues about masculinities.

The most extensive debate has concerned the concept of hegemonic masculinity. This idea originated in research in schools, as a way of understanding the relations between different patterns of masculinity and the overall gender regime of the school. But it has found much wider application.

'Hegemonic masculinity' means the pattern of social conduct by men, or associated with the social position of men, which is most honoured, which occupies a central position in a structure of gender relations, and which helps to stabilize an unequal gender order as a whole. Especially, hegemonic masculinity confirms and enables the social and economic advantages of men *in general* over women. Crucially, this pattern of masculinity is distinguished not only from femininity, but also from the subordinated or marginalized masculinities that exist in the same society.

The concept of hegemonic masculinity thus relies on the research evidence that there are multiple masculinities; that different masculinities have unequal authority or social legitimacy; and that men and masculinity are usually privileged over women and femininity. The concept has been widely debated. My colleague James Messerschmidt and I published a review of this debate some years ago, proposing improvements to the concept.[7]

The concept of masculinities has often been simplified into a psychological typology. That's an easy slippage, because everyone is accustomed to talking about mental or cultural types – the introverted, Generation X, etc. But when we look closely at how gender hierarchies work, such an approach won't do. Gender and gender inequalities involve complex social patterns of centrality and marginality. Race, class and sexuality all have an impact. So does culture and region. For instance, the masculinity that is hegemonic at a local level may be significantly different from the hegemonic masculinity at a regional or global level – though there is usually some overlap.

Violence is in the background of these discussions, but is easily misunderstood. I think it currently is misunderstood in media talk about 'toxic masculinity'.

The term 'toxic masculinity' has come into use in journalism quite recently, especially in the USA as a result of the #MeToo movement. There are certainly gender patterns in violent and abusive behaviour. Sexual harassment is widely experienced by women – in workplaces, and in public places – and it mainly comes from men. Some men experience sexual harassment; their numbers are smaller. Rape is a very persistent and widespread form of violence and is mainly by men targeting women, though some rapes target men. Domestic violence in the form of killings and violent assault is mainly of women by men. Homophobic murders are mainly done by men; in this case it is mainly men who are targeted, though some women are. There are other forms of violence by men in which mainly men are targeted. War was the classic example, before the development of strategic bombing and nuclear weapons which vaporize women and men equally.

Given these patterns, it is understandable why some people speak of 'toxic masculinity'. But we cannot assume that a fixed type of masculinity is a simple cause of violence. Modern criminology doesn't see the matter that way. Rather, it pays attention to the social circumstances in which violence can be used to construct masculinity and claim a position in the world.[8] Violent and abusive behaviour often have links with economic and institutional inequalities between women and men. Some patterns of violence are linked with cultural definitions of manhood – for instance physical confrontations in public places, or the way military forces have developed rhetorics of masculinity to keep their forces from breaking up. Homophobic violence is often done by groups of men who form an audience for each other.

Hegemonic masculinity does *not* equate to violent masculinity. A man who needs a gun to assert himself is not in a hegemonic position – he may have power but not legitimacy. Yet violence matters for hegemony. Guns in the hands of police or soldiers may, and often do, back up authority: they reinforce consent by making consent the prudent option. Antonio Gramsci, the Italian revolutionary who developed the modern concept of hegemony, spoke of society's 'common sense' as a vehicle of hegemony. And in everyday mass culture, there is a great deal of masculinized violence and displays of force. Consider the prevalence of violent sports, Hollywood thrillers, television cop shows, military parades, and images of war. Generals notoriously die in bed; but a lot of their troops die on the front line, and die young.

IV Thinking on a world scale

When the diversity of masculinities became apparent, some way of ordering them became necessary. A narrative of progress was one way to do this. A 'traditional' masculinity (often understood as patriarchal) was contrasted with a 'modern' masculinity (supposed more egalitarian). Mass media are often happy with this schema, especially when patriarchal masculinities can be folded into the image of bearded Islamist terrorists.

The crude propaganda function of such ideas can't be overlooked. But a more important problem with this kind of thinking has been pointed out by the South African psychologist Kopano Ratele. As he observes, it is a mistake to think that 'tradition' is uniform and always patriarchal. Traditions about gender are multiple, and are constantly being re-negotiated. Some traditions are indeed patriarchal but others are democratic and inclusive. Tradition offers resources for gender equality, too.[9]

We should abandon the idea that the world is divided into 'modern' and 'pre-modern' cultures. Latin American thinkers especially argue that we are all part of one modernity – a world modernity, where the European and North American story is one thread in a larger pattern. In this perspective it was *imperialism*, not capitalism or the industrial revolution, that was the driving force of global modernity. And imperialism was (and is) a strongly gendered process. Colonial conquest was carried out by masculinized workforces. Colonial society smashed or transformed existing gender orders around the world, creating distinctive new gender arrangements, not simply reproducing those of the imperial centre. Consider, for instance, the importance of race in the gender barriers of colonial societies. The colonial and post-colonial dynamics of masculinity are now seen as an important problem.

This question too has a history. In 1952 the first book by a young psychiatrist and war veteran from Martinique was published in Paris.[10] Its publication went almost unnoticed at the time, but the author, Frantz Fanon, later became an icon of third world revolt. *Black Skin, White Masks* is a brilliant, troubling analysis of the psychology of racism in France and its colonial empire. The book is also an analysis of white and black masculinities. Fanon is clear that colonialism is a system of violence and economic exploitation – with psychological consequences. Within that structure, black masculinity is marked by divided emotions, and a massive alienation from original experience. This alienation is produced as black men struggle to find a position, and find recognition, in a culture that defines them as biologically inferior, indeed a kind of animal, and makes them objects of anxiety or fear.

Thirty years later, similar themes were picked up by the Indian psychologist Ashis Nandy in another remarkable book, *The Intimate Enemy*.[11] Nandy wrote about British rather than French colonialism, but like Fanon he tried to combine cultural and psychological analysis with a realistic view of imperialism. Nandy analyses, through brilliant case studies, masculinities among both the colonized and the colonizers. He argues that their dynamics are closely linked. Colonialism tends to exaggerate gender hierarchies, and to produce simplified, power-oriented masculinities among the colonizers. There is historical research from other parts of the British empire that supports this view.

There is now a considerable body of research and thought from the postcolonial world about men and masculinities. It highlights the long-term effects of colonization, the impact of racial hierarchies, and the cultural and psychological consequences of economic dependence.[12] In Latin America, for instance, there have been important discussions of the impact of neoliberal restructuring on masculinity and patriarchal fatherhood. As the attempts to create balanced, autonomous economies were replaced by a focus on profitable exports into global markets, many working-class men's jobs vanished and employment became more precarious. The 'breadwinner' model of working-class masculinity became unsustainable. In the Arab world, researchers documented cultural turbulence about masculinity resulting from cultural and economic domination by Europe and North America, long after formal independence. The search for viable new forms of masculinity has fuelled both democratic and authoritarian movements.

The postcolonial world not only gives us a richer picture of masculinities, obliging us to think of different dynamics of change. It also challenges our concepts and frames of thought. We are now in a position to consider alternatives to Northern dominance in many areas of knowledge.

Critiques of Northern dominance include postcolonial theory, whose best-known practitioner was Edward Said; the decolonial approach, focussed on Latin America; and attempts to form multi-centred knowledge practices. An important movement has emphasized the value of indigenous knowledges, marginalized by colonialism, as locally-based alternatives to the dominant international positivist knowledge system. But we also need to consider the intellectuals of colonial and postcolonial societies who work from the experience of *new* social forms. My overview in *Southern Theory* calls attention to the creativity and power of their intellectual work, and the importance of the historical experience of colonial and postcolonial societies.[13]

Masculinity research is one field that needs this approach. Gender research in the global North has generally presumed a coherent gender order with continuity through time – for instance in concepts like 'patriarchy'. But this assumption cannot be made for *colonial* societies, with their history of massive violence and disruption; nor for many parts of today's postcolonial South, where cultural discontinuity and disruption is the condition of life. In such conditions a dominant masculinity may not be 'hegemonic', because no settled hegemony is possible.[14]

With this in mind, we should think of gender hegemony not as an automatic process, but as a historical *project* undertaken by different social groups at different times. Even where some hegemony has been established, it is possible to challenge it.

A progressive challenge is illustrated by the proposals for engaged fatherhood in Scandinavia – given a material form in paternal-leave laws – and *paternidad afectiva* in Latin America. But social change is not all in one direction. It is also possible to promote a more power-oriented, sexist masculinity. Something like that has happened with the rise of authoritarian populism, featuring displays of a hard masculinity from leaders like Putin, Trump and Modi.

If we are looking for the elite levels of masculine power in today's world, we have to go beyond the spectacle of politics to the gritty world of economics. Especially to the transnational corporations that are now our dominant economic institutions. They include the banks, hedge funds and financial brokers, the oil, coal and gas companies, the tech giants, the bulk transport firms, the great property trusts and the armaments manufacturers.

This is a heavily masculinized social world – over 95% of the CEOs of large transnational corporations are men. The few women have to 'manage like a man'. There is some research on managerial masculinities, though it is difficult to get access to the very top levels. What strikes me most strongly is the collectivism of managerial work, which is often tightly integrated into corporate intranets, and subject to constant surveillance. It is a pressured, competitive, and unforgiving world. A high level of gender conformity is not surprising. Though managers can be tolerant of limited sexual diversity (for instance, including gay men in transnational managerial roles), we should not expect any major movement from them towards gender equality. Capitalism doesn't work that way.

V Luther's paradox
We can now refine Yeats' observation. Godhead is commonly perceived as masculine in a social and cultural context where power and authority are understood as masculine. But not any kind of masculine. Familiar images of God draw specifically on hegemonic constructions of masculinity – and not just in the benevolent bourgeois grandfather pictured on Sunday School cards. Consider, for instance, the forbidding images of royal power in Byzantine mosaics of Christ Pantokrator; or the hyper-masculine figure of wrath that Michelangelo painted at the centre of the altar wall in the Sistine Chapel.

Since hegemonic masculinities are based on the subordination of other masculinities, it's not surprising that patriarchal religions police expressions of masculinity. Right now, both Catholic and Protestant fundamentalists are engaged in campaigns against 'gender ideology' or 'gender theory', by which they mean any suggestion that masculinities and femininities are plural, or alterable, or that the relationship between them is negotiable. Particular targets are gay and trans groups. In the background, the campaign is directed against feminist women and their demands for equality.

Michelangelo's contemporary Martin Luther never challenged the legitimacy of earthly power; famously, he opposed the peasants' rebellion of 1524–25. But he certainly didn't think the rich and powerful were themselves admirable. His Preface to the *Magnificat* was written at a crucial moment in the Reformation and addressed to a powerful duke, one of the German aristocrats then lining up to support the reformer. In this text he wrote of the experience of a God 'who sees into the depths, and gives help only to the poor, the despised, the pitiable, the sorrowing, the forsaken, and those of no account'[16]

– a God who frequently chastises kings, and chooses Mary *because* she is poor, unknown, of no account. Luther's whole doctrine of justification has this flavour; it subverts the earthly hierarchies from which Martin himself could never break.

That's part of a long tradition of radical thought within religion, from St Francis, through the Anabaptists and the Quakers, to liberation theology, Ambedkar's Buddhism and Shariati's Islamic thought. That tradition should be borne in mind as well as the tradition of misogyny I mentioned at the start. The construction of missionary masculinities was part of the building of global empires, undermining pre-conquest gender orders and indigenous religions – the burning of the Maya books in Yucatan by the missionary bishop Diego de Landa in 1562 is a famous episode. But no campaign to impose gender order or cultural uniformity has succeeded in the long run, as the multiplicity of masculinities in the world today bears witness.

The following papers in this issue of *Concilium* will go much deeper into these questions; I can only hope this brief introduction to the field of research suggests some useful directions. It is not a topic that everyone finds comfortable. When I was awarded my first grant for research on masculinities, it was denounced by a right-wing parliamentary committee in Australia as a waste of public funds. I think they were wrong, and not just because this research has clear applications in education, health and welfare. We need to understand masculinities and pay attention to the dynamics of men's lives if we are, in the long run, to achieve gender justice.

Notes

1. 'Ribh Denounces Patrick', in W.B. Yeats, *Collected Poems*, London: Macmillan, 1950, p. 328.
2. The emergence of the field is traced in more detail in Raewyn Connell, *Masculinities*, second edition, Cambridge: Polity Press, 2005.
3. Octavio Paz, *The Labyrinth of Solitude*, enlarged edition, London: Penguin, 1990 [1950].
4. Sigrid Metz-Göckel and Ursula Müller, *Der Mann: Die BRIGITTE-Studie*, Hamburg: Beltz, 1985.
5. For this document and its downstream, see *The Role of Men and Boys in Achieving Gender Equality*, 'Women 2000 and Beyond' series, New York: United Nations Division for the Advancement of Women/ Department of Economic and Social Affairs, http.www.un.org/womenwatch/daw/w2000.html.
6. Teresa Valdés and José Olavarría (eds), *Masculinidades y equidad de género en America Latina*, Santiago: FLACSO-Chile, 1998.
7. Raewyn Connell and James W. Messerschmidt, 'Hegemonic Masculinity: Rethinking the Concept', *Gender and Society*, 19.6 (2005), 829–859.
8. For the pioneering statement see James W. Messerschmidt, *Masculinities and Crime*, Lanham: Rowman & Littlefield.
9. Kopano Ratele, 'Masculinities without Tradition', *Politikon: South African Journal of Political Studies*, 40.1 (2013), 133–156.
10. Franz Fanon, Black Skin, White Masks, New York: Grove Press, 1967 [1952].
11. Ashis Nandy, *The Intimate Enemy: Loss and Recovery of Self under Colonialism*, Delhi: Oxford University Press, 1983.
12. For a recent collection see Mangesh Kulkarni (ed), *Global Masculinities: Interrogations and Reconstructions*, Abingdon: Routledge, 2019.
13. Raewyn Connell, *Southern Theory: The Global Dynamics of Knowledge in Social Science*, Cambridge: Polity Press, 2007.
14. Raewyn Connell, 'Margin becoming centre: for a world-centred rethinking of masculinities', *NORMA: International Journal for Masculinity Studies*, 9.4 (2014), 217–231.
15. Sarah Bracke and David Paternotte, 'Unpacking the Sin of Gender', *Religion & Gender*, 6.2 (2016), 143–154.
16. Martin Luther, *Reformation Writings*, translated by Bertram L. Woolf, vol. 2, London: 1956, pp. 192–193.

A Theology for Reimagining Masculinities

HERBERT ANDERSON

The new era of more fluid, expansive, non-binary understandings of being human presents a challenge to Christian theology's reluctance to address the enduring primacy of masculine images of God to maintain gender hierarchies subordinating women. The present global crisis, evidenced by 'strongman' politics, sex trafficking, and sexual harassment of women by high-profile men, is the consequence of toxic masculinity that persists in patriarchal systems. This essay proposes a theological framework for reimagining masculinity that challenges patriarchy, encourages humility in language about God, invites men to grieve their losses and embraces human and divine vulnerability as a necessary corrective to hegemonic masculinity.

I Introduction

The history of Christian theology is replete with images and pronouncements that promote patriarchy, valorize masculine pre-eminence, and subjugate women to a status inferior to men. Such perspectives have changed and are changing slowly as a consequence of an emerging understanding of gender fluidity that has replaced old binaries of gender. The intersectionality of gender with wealth and race has simultaneously complicated the process and intensified the need for change. Conversely, freedom for more nuanced gender identities will be enhanced by religious contexts that challenge gender hierarchies.

Christian theologians have been slow to challenge the reigning presumptions about masculinity, even as feminist theologians have posed nuanced and sophisticated analyses of the impact of gendered language on

Christian thought and practice. This essay challenges persistent patriarchal images of male dominance within Christian theology and practice. Raewyn Connell, in the first essay in this volume of *Concilium*, says:

> 'Godhead is commonly perceived as masculine in a social and cultural context where power and authority are understood as masculine […]. Since hegemonic masculinities are based on the subordination of other masculinities, it is not surprising that patriarchal religions police expressions of masculinity.'

The reluctance to rethink masculinity is sustained not only by intractable male images of God but also by the promotion of human dominion over creation; dualisms that persist in patriarchal social institutions based in essentialist understandings of the human being limit our exploration of multiple masculinities. Such dualisms are contexts of patriarchal violence. It is incumbent on Christian theologians to redress enduring presumptions of male pre-eminence that continue to support hegemonic masculinity.

II The urgent need for change
This essay is in two parts. The first part describes the persistence of hegemonic masculinity as a global reality and the consequent difficulty in embracing new and more just expressions of masculinities that are not simplistically opposed to femininities or structured in a dominant relationship with femininities. The second half of the essay proposes some themes for a theological framework for emerging masculinities. In every region around the world, 'strongman' leaders continue to dominate with unchallenged power. These strongmen feed on cycles of fear and their political power that supports the reproduction of male dominance and privilege in the household, in the marketplace and in the political arena. Both women and men are casualties of this continuing crisis. Worldwide sexual trafficking also confirms that women continue to be violated and abused to satisfy male desire for sexual gratification and power.

The HIV crisis in sub-Sahara Africa is generally regarded as a gendered epidemic, supported by patriarchal constructions of masculinity, commonly characterized by power, potency, sexual aggression, and fertility. In response to the HIV epidemic, African feminist theologians pointed to patriarchy as the root problem for masculinities that became deadly in the context of HIV.[1] This crisis, however, is not unique to African societies. Countries and cultures in which human trafficking and other forms of emotional and physical violence toward women persist need to identify a similar mandate to address toxic masculinity embedded in patriarchal systems. Patriarchal cultures incubate toxic masculinity.

When a significant number of women in the United States, empowered by the #MeToo movement, exposed patterns of sexual harassment and abuse by high-profile men, male claims to power and privilege were publicly challenged. As a result, male dominance and abuse is no longer simply personal and private, confined to family or the workplace and tolerated secretly by women. It is now also public and political. Despite all the changes in men that have occurred over the last five decades, patriarchal assumptions linger and male patterns of control and domination and consequent violence persist. The sexual abuse and sexual harassment of women is simply another exercise of male power and the desire to dominate. Even more alarming are the connections that have been made between domestic violence and mass shootings. In more than half of the mass shootings between 2009 and 2017, an intimate partner or family member has been an intended victim. The current social and political climate in the United States has given some men permission to reclaim old, damaging patterns of patriarchy or link a toxic masculinity with racial anxiety to support white male primacy. The articulation of alternatives to these old destructive stereotypes is an urgent matter for the sake of a human future.

III Challenges to reimagining masculinities

Reimagining masculinity for our time is as complicated as it is urgent. Assumptions of privilege and patterns of abuse have endured so long that men still believe that it is their nature to dominate. Having physical power made male domination easy, but it also defined what it meant to be a man. Men ploughed fields, fought wars, built railroads, dug graves, and forged steel because they were physically strong. Emotional strength was neither necessary nor encouraged. The ideology of patriarchy has endured long after physical prowess was the occasion for male dominance. When power came to be understood as the capacity to influence or have an effect, psychological power replaced physical strength for men in the exercise of control. Subsequent definitions of being a man not only favoured dominance and independence and self-control but also control over people, social realities, and physical resources.

As Raewyn Connell defines it, the hegemonic ideal of masculinity includes not only behaviour toward women but also hierarchies of men arranged and marginalized in relation to the dominant male gender stereotype. Hegemonic masculinity helped me understand a damaging lifelong pattern of comparing myself to other men whom I determined were really masculine because they were more taciturn, more self-assured, self-contained, less vulnerable, more aggressive, more sexually potent. A personal story illustrates this point: Some years ago, while I was still teaching at Catholic Theological Union in Chicago, I announced to a class that my wife had just accepted a position at Seattle University and that I would follow her career for a second time and move to Seattle. In response to this announcement, a young student blurted out: 'You're a wuss.' It was a clear declaration that in his world view I did not embody hegemonic masculinity.

For the student, I suspect my decision was a violation of the unspoken masculine code about headship, dominance, and control. I was already aware of my low status on the masculine hierarchy whenever men would say to me 'I couldn't do what you do' in response to learning that I was the primary cook in the family. The unspoken message was 'you shouldn't either!'

Any time of transition is notoriously chaotic. The present challenges to male dominance are no exception. When traditional male values are challenged and as more elastic visions of gender emerge, some men say they are confused. Other men feel betrayed by social progress that has created uncertainty for them about what it means to be a man. They have not experienced the challenge to male dominance over the last decades as beneficial to their well-being or success. Dismantling hegemonic hierarchies that abuse and marginalize other men will be a uniquely challenging agenda in reimagining masculinities.

IV A theological framework for multiple masculinities

Ongoing attempts to diminish the male dominance of biblical, liturgical, and theological language have made progress but a gap remains between the traditional male-dominated imagery used on Sunday worship or common Christian practice and what theologians regard as inclusive language necessary for gender justice. This chasm was evident when Christian theologians and church leaders in the sub-Sahara African nations challenged the structures of patriarchy that funded destructive male behaviour in the HIV crisis. They agreed that patriarchy was the problem: they did not agree on the solution. Conservative African churches favoured reforming masculinity within a patriarchal framework (preserving notions like male headship and male responsibility) while African feminist theologians insisted on transforming masculinity beyond patriarchy. That difference is replicated among those who may agree that toxic masculinity is a problem. If Raewyn Connell's observation that 'familiar images of God draw specifically on hegemonic constructions of masculinity' is correct, and I believe it is, the challenge to fashion a new and more inclusive theological framework for masculinities is both essential and daunting. This essay suggests some dimensions of a theological framework to support reimagining masculinity in a less hierarchical, more inclusive way.

1) Toxic masculinity will not be transformed unless patriarchy is diminished.

More than three decades ago, feminist theologian Mary Daly identified the connection between Christianity and patriarchy with a single line that has almost become a cliché: 'If God is male, then male is God.'[2] Despite abstract formulations that insist God is beyond gender and neither male nor female, most of the names and images of God have been drawn from the world of ruling men. God as Father, as Lord, as Divine King and Ruler, as absolute Monarch who is omnipotent and unmoved are all images that reinforce male privilege and domination. Rehabilitating masculinities while preserving patriarchy may generate a kinder, gentler patriarchy but it is still patriarchy. Therefore, the challenge for theologians is to purge Christian theology of deeply rooted ideologies of patriarchy and promote masculinities that forego notions of dominance, and presumptions of privilege.

2) Eliminating patriarchy from social institutions is particularly prob-lematic.
Social institutions are susceptible to embedding hierarchies that undermine human well-being for their participants. For example, Frank J. Barrett has described how naval officers used hegemonic categories of independence, aggression, and risk-taking to create a hierarchy of masculinities with aviators at the top and supply officers at the bottom.[3] In a challenging essay in *The Atlantic*, James Carroll links the continuance of celibate clericalism in the Roman Catholic Church with theological misogyny that excludes women from the priesthood and preserves male power.[4] Moreover, paedophilia and decades of ecclesiastical cover-up within a rigid male hierarchy embodies hegemonic masculinity's crime against young men. The reform of the Catholic Church, as James Carroll envisions it, must include the end of male dominance. James Carroll has it right. The theological challenge for all Christian communions (including Roman Catholicism) is to redefine the Church without perpetuating its patriarchal underpinnings. The redemption of hierarchies begins with empathy and the recognition of commonality despite the differences that separate and reinforce the impulse to marginalize.

3) Adding feminine images to traditional language for God is a useful transition but insufficient long-term goal. Some Christian denominations have mandated the use of feminine as well as masculine images for God in worship. For example, the Lord's Prayer is addressed to 'our Father and our Mother in Heaven'. New hymns include feminine images for God. God is still gendered but imaged as both feminine and masculine. Thinking of God as feminine may be a helpful or even necessary transition out of a male, patriarchal father God but it will not help us discover vulnerability or tenderness or nurturing in men that we also know in God. Traits like nurturing, intimacy, vulnerability can and should be considered as masculine – or even better, as human – traits and not as feminine traits to be borrowed by men. The incarnation reveals a loving God whose care for humankind is so great that God was and is willing to risk everything for loving the world.

4) Words and symbols about the mystery of God and the mystery of being human begin in humility. Although we cannot not speak of God, we begin all speaking of God with humility. God who is always more than we can know. Moreover, God cannot be tied to any name. God is the unspeakable and unknowable I AM who transcends all categories. Language that restricts God to male images is idolatrous. Humility is appropriate for our language about God and it is equally significant for descriptions of the human person. Descriptors of men that tilt toward an essentialist perspective diminish mystery by supporting a narrower view of being human. The mythopoetic movement in the last decade of the 20th century attempted to rehabilitate masculinity with ancient archetypes like king, warrior, magician, and lover. I proposed four additional images that have their roots in a Christian understanding of being human: sage, peacemaker, gardener, and friend. If we begin with humility, then many names, many images, many adjectives can be used to refer to both divine and human being. God as the Holy One is nurturing, vulnerable, patient, generative, compassionate, creative, courageous, determined, loving. These same descriptors become emerging masculinities for the many selves of men.

5) Fostering open-hearted and just regard for multiple masculinities and establishing a just bond between women and men are mutually interdependent. The positive changes made in the larger society and in many marriages today have not eliminated injustice from marriage or eradicated injustice toward women in the church and at work. Nor have patterns of discrimination and injustice among men been eliminated. Equal regard among men and an equitable redistribution of power between women and men are reciprocally connected. Gender justice redistributes power and seeks to eliminate oppression between men and women and among men. If it can be established that gender equality is in everyone's interest, then men will be more likely to join with women in working toward the goal of gender justice. Even so, equal pay for equal work, as one expression of gender justice, may be mandated before it is internalized. Gender justice is first of all a vision.

6) It is both difficult and necessary for men to acknowledge the unspoken grief they feel for the loss of privilege or unimpaired power or job security. Because grief for what men have lost has not always been accorded moral standing, it was buried and became a major source of smoldering resentment among many men. The strategies for diminishing male dominance or violence have been ineffective in part because the patriarchal heart has not been transformed from within. Rita Nakashima Brock has proposed the image of 'broken-heartedness' as one approach for transforming male dominance and the abuse of power.[5] It is not enough, she argues, to disrupt patriarchy and privilege. Before hearts can be tutored, they must be healed. Before a heart can be healed, there must be a recognized need for healing. For men, this begins by admitting that the patriarchal heart is fearful and broken and full of hidden grief. The agenda for the modern men is not easy: to mourn their losses while imagining a new future without the presumptions of privilege and power they once enjoyed.

7) The capacity to embrace the interdependence of all creatures is a corrective to domination in every form. The misinterpretation of the creation narratives not only promoted male dominion over female human beings, it also fostered a hierarchy of the human one over creation. Under this rubric, dominion and domination were supported as appropriate patterns of human activity. If, however, we understand creation as a complex ecosystem in which the human, animals, and plants all mingle together interdependently, then there is little justification for dominion. All things belong to God. Interdependence is the norm. The relationship of mutuality between men and women, between men and other men, and between men and creation mirrors the interdependence of all things.

8) Discovering and embracing multiple expressions of masculine humanness is more likely if men embody a paradoxical posture between knowing and not-knowing, between being on the way to fuller humanity and not being there yet. In Christian theology, the Cross embodies the paradoxical presence of power and vulnerability in divine as well as in human life. The One whose power fashioned the universe entered human life as a vulnerable infant and was willingly executed in a humiliating death. The crucifixion of Jesus is the crossing of power and vulnerability for the sake of freedom and compassion. Sam Keen says it well in *Fire in the Belly*:

> 'The image of Jesus on the Cross is central to the Christian notion of manhood because it dramatizes the issue of will, a recurring theme in any discussion of manhood. [...] The lesson of Gethsemane is that a man is most virile not when he insists upon his autonomous will but when he harmonizes his will with the will of God.'[6]

The boldness and virility of Jesus will seem far away from men today if they understand autonomy as self-will or self-preservation or winning rather than obedience to the will of God. If, however, men embody the contradictions of the Cross by holding on and letting go, by acting and being acted upon, by embracing ambiguity with certainty, by noting the unexpected crossing moments of daily dying, by leaving the door to the soul ajar to be surprised by God, they will exercise power while embracing vulnerability.

9) Sharing power and acknowledging vulnerability are unavoidable dimensions in reimagining masculinity.
I came to that conviction the hard way. I had learned early in my marriage about sharing power for the sake of justice. Then, in May 1999, I was diagnosed with prostate cancer, and I became aware of vulnerability in a new way. Having prostate cancer was a tangible reminder to me that men are susceptible to being wounded at the locus of their sexual power. Prostate cancer (or the fear of it) touches deeply the masculine centre of power for most men. This connection between power and vulnerability in the male anatomy is a useful metaphor for reimagining an alternative to hegemonic masculinity. I have explored this theme more fully in my reprinted book *Jacob's Shadow: Reimagining Masculinity*.[7] In the ancient myths, men presumed power without vulnerability. What we know more clearly today is that men (and women) are in fact most powerful when they acknowledge and act out of human vulnerability and most vulnerable when presuming the invulnerability of their power.

10) In order to redeem hegemonic masculinity, the language we use to speak of God should balance images of power with metaphors of vulnerability.

The manly ideal, Dorothee Soelle has observed, is opposed by the Crucified Christ. 'The masculine myth of the invulnerable hero is opposed to the unarmed carpenter's son from Galilee: there is nothing here to harmonize.'[8] Some approaches to the Christian faith emphasize invulnerability and success as signs of God's presence but they are false promises that can only be sustained by also denying the abundance of suffering in the world. Insisting on an all-powerful God who promises prosperity is a human temptation when we feel powerless. We need to learn to live consciously with human and divine vulnerability as one hope for the transformation of hegemonic masculinity.

V A heuristic postscript
Until recently, gender construction has been determined mostly by a simplistic sense of biology. We now understand more clearly how gender is both ascribed and learned; biology itself complicates any simple sense of gender in both human and animal worlds. The new era of non-binary, gender fluid, gender expansive descriptions of being human will vary inevitably cross cultures. Even so, the Christian story offers one universal liberating perspective despite its history of misogyny and male domination. The defining metaphors for the human one in relation to God are gender neutral. Being a 'child of God' transcends gender. Sainthood is not gender specific. Nor is discipleship dependent on preserving gendered distinctions. And because of God's incarnation, hegemonic masculinity is a 'non-essential luxury'.

I am indebted to W.H. Auden's Christmas verse drama *For the Time Being* for an alternative expression of masculinity. Although the biblical narrative does not tell how or when Joseph was informed of Mary's pregnancy for which he was not responsible, Auden imagines the consequence of this startling news for Joseph: 'Today the roles are altered; you must be the Weaker Sex whose passion is passivity.'[9] Joseph is given no reason or proof that Mary's pregnancy is God's will. He must simply believe and 'choose what is difficult as if it were easy.' Auden's description of what Joseph (and so all men) must give up reads like a clinical definition of toxic masculinity.

'For those delicious memories
Cigars and sips of brandy can restore
To old, dried boys, for gallantry that scrawls
In idolatrous detail and size
A symbol of aggression on toilet walls,
For having reasoned – "woman is naturally pure
Since she has no moustache," for having said
"No woman has a business head."
You must learn now that masculinity,
To Nature, is a non-essential luxury.'

W.H. Auden's creative rendering of God's Incarnation does not eliminate human biology nor does it eradicate the necessity of socially constructed roles for men and women.

'Forgetting nothing and believing all,
You must behave as if this were not strange at all.
Without a change in look or word,
You both must act exactly as before;
Joseph and Mary shall be man and wife
Just as if nothing had occurred.'

In Joseph, traditional masculinity was transformed. He acted justly, gently, bravely, selflessly so that the mystery of the incarnation could unfold. Had this been an early interpretation of Joseph, the Christian story might have championed the liberation of men from hegemonic domination and presumed patriarchal privilege from the beginning. In that moment and for Joseph's life, traditional masculinity was transformed and no longer necessary. In so doing, Joseph provides a new and liberating vision of multiple masculinities 'as if it were not strange at all.'

Notes

1. Adriaan S. van Klinken, 'Theology, Gender Ideology and Masculinity Politics: A Discussion on the Transformation of Masculinities as Envisioned by African Theologians and a Local Pentecostal Church', *Journal of Theology for Southern Africa*, 138 (2010), 2–18.
2. Mary Daly, *Beyond God the Father: Toward a Philosophy of Woman's Liberation*, Beacon Press: Boston, 1973, p. 19.
3. Frank J. Barrett, 'The Organizational Construction of Hegemonic Masculinity: The Case of the US Navy', *Gender, Work and Organization*, 3.3 (1996), 129–142.
4. James Carroll, 'Abolish the Priesthood: To Save the Catholic Church, Return it to the People', *The Atlantic*, 323.3 (2019), 76–84.
5. Rita Nakashima Brock, *Journeys by Heart: A Christology of Erotic Power*, New York: Crossroad, 1989, p. xv.
6. Sam Keen, *Fire in the Belly: On Being a Man*, New York: Bantom Books, 1991, p. 102.
7. Herbert Anderson, *Jacob's Shadow: Reimagining Masculinity*, reprint, Eugene:Wipf & Stock, 2019.
8. Dorothee Soelle, *Window of Vulnerability: A Political Spirituality*, translated by Linda M. Maloney, Minneapolis: Fortress, 1990, p. xi.
9. W.H. Auden, *Collected Poems*, edited by Edward Mendelson, New York: Vintage International, 1991, pp. 364–365

Part Two: Masculinity Between Religion, Politics and Culture

Masculinity Undone: Reading Mark 14.51–52 from *El Otro Lado*

MANUEL VILLALOBOS MENDOZA

*What did it mean to be manly or masculine in the New Testament world? To be a 'man' or a 'woman' had little to do with biology in Greco-Roman culture. A man must perform and demonstrate his masculinity always, in order to be deemed as a 'real man' (*verus vir*). Thus, it is unusual that Mark 14.51–52 presents a young man whose masculinity is at odds with social norms during Jesus's arrest. His youthfulness as well as his luxurious linen garment (*sindōn) reveals his identity as* effeminatus. *Moreover, his naked body and running away cowardly in the middle of the night, demonstrate his inability to prove his masculinity.*

I Introduction

For biblical scholars, it is almost an obligation nowadays to 'come out' in the biblical field in order to disclose their social location. In my situation, I have resisted the temptation to describe myself as Latino or Hispanic due to the ambiguity of both terms. Thus, I have created a hermeneutic which may embrace my 'otherness' as well as my denied existence due to my race, economical situation and sexual orientation. In Mexico people that deviate from heteronormative practices and are incapable to perform correctly a 'toxic masculinity' are mercilessly situated into the non-existence of *el otro lado* ('the other side'). Consequently, my hermeneutic is called a hermeneutic *del otro lado*.

I have described elsewhere how this hermeneutic *del otro lado* privileges questions and voices of otherness, masculinity, marginality, gender,

39

sexuality, sexual orientation, ethnicity, economics, and the borderland in the biblical text and my biblical interpretation.[1] Some of these concerns will be obvious in my approach to Mark 14.51–52, where the author narrates a very rare scene during Jesus' arrest:

> 'A certain young man was following him, wearing nothing but a linen cloth. They caught hold of him, but he left the linen cloth and ran off naked' (NRSV).

In this article, I am primarily concerned with how Mark exposes this young man to our gaze and situates him in a dangerous arena where conflicting issues of masculinity are present. I do not attempt any assessment of textual historicity here. My interpretation *del otro lado* does not care if this young man was a historical character or a creation of the author. I am concerned in this article how the textual construction of this young man's masculinity may challenges other textual constructions of masculinity in the Greco-Roman culture of the first century, contemporary to Mark's gospel. Thus, I use the categories of 'virile' and 'effeminate' as they were understood in the Greco-Roman culture of the first century. These categories do not necessarily reflect our own understanding nowadays of 'masculinity'.

In antiquity (as today?), to be a 'real man' (*verus vir*) was understood primarily in terms of the relationship of power between penetrator and penetrated. A 'real man' was the one who penetrates another body, whether a female, a boy, an 'effeminate' man, or a slave.[2] The rule of masculinity thus was simple and well demarcated: to penetrate another and never be penetrated. In this struggle of power and dominance, the Romans saw themselves as the 'impenetrable penetrators';[3] the others were just the opposite, the shameful, the abjected, and the effeminate body.

If these were the rules regarding masculinity and 'being a real man' in antiquity, I wonder why Mark 14.51 depicts a young man running naked in the middle of the night? Is this the proper behaviour of a *verus vir*, as constructed in Mark's Greco-Roman context? What is the relationship of this young man with Jesus? Is Mark's community subverting or redefining the notion of masculinity of their contemporary society? What might be the implications for us today, especially for all those who have suffered from a 'toxic' masculinity? These are some of the questions I will address in this article.

II Young and beautiful?: Masculinity at risk!

Mark describes him as *neaniskos* (young man). This term will appear again in Mark 16.5, where the young man appears wearing a long white robe and explains to the women why Jesus's body is not found in the tomb. It is interesting that in their obsession to reveal the historical identity of this enigmatic young naked man, scholars have paid little attention to issues of masculinity which, from my hermeneutic *del otro lado* are so evident and attractive. Biblical scholars have offered a plethora of interpretations about this young man:

> 'Some regard him as real historical figure, one of Jesus' own disciples (John the son of Zebedee, James the Lord's brother, or John Mark, understood to be the evangelist himself), or a curious neighbour aroused from sleep who gets swept up into the confusion surrounding the arrest. Others take the "naked man" to be an angel (see 16:5), a symbol for Jesus himself, or even a symbol for the Christian undergoing baptismal initiation.'[4]

The identity of the *neaniskos* has not been – and likely will never be – resolved. And yet, Mark invites us to gaze upon this young naked body and challenges us to reflect whether he could be judged a *verus vir* or should be classified as a deviant *effeminatus*. The text, while short, offers several indicators that raise this question, especially when read on the background of other textual constructions of masculinity in antiquity.

Greek writers use the term *neaniskos* to describe a man who is at the height of youthful vigour and strength. The term *neaniskos* is a flexible category that could refer to a young man between 24 and 40 years old. Being a *neaniskos* was (is?) not an easy age for the *veri viri*, because they could easily lose their virility and suffer from the unmanly disease of effemination due to their emotional instability and other 'womanish' forms of behaviour. The young men, who in some contexts are portrayed as vigorous, beautiful, and bursting with sex-appeal, can also be viewed, by older men, as wilful, greedy, ambitious, sex-crazed, and emotionally unstable. For moralists, philosophers, and rhetoricians, these characteristics and behaviours are unbecoming to men and render the young men 'effeminate':

'Look at our young men: they are lazy, their intellects asleep; no one can stay awake to take pain over a single honest pursuit. Sleep, torpor and a perseverance in evil that is more shameful than either have seized hold of their minds. Libidinous delight in song and dance transfixes these effeminates. Braiding the hair, refining the voice till it is as caressing as a woman's, competing in bodily softness with women, beautifying themselves with filthy fineries – this is the pattern our youths set themselves' (Seneca, *Controversiae*, 1 praefatio 8).

III Wearing the (un)manly toga

But being a *neaniskos*, with its connotations of problematic behaviours, was not the only threat against Mark's young man's masculinity. The *sindōn* or 'soft linen garment' that this *neaniskos* is wearing in Mark's text, can also be read as an ambivalent signifier of gender. Clothing is language, as Tertullian says: 'Even if utterance is mute [...] my very clothing speaks' (*De pallio* 6.1.1). And clothing speaks particularly loudly about gender. It distinguishes the real man from the effeminate, honour from shame, active from passive, top from bottom. As a primary signifier of the gendered body, dress was an essential, means of constructing, maintaining, and negotiating these 'masculine' categories. So we can ask: What does the *neaniskos*'s *sindōn* say? Does the *sindōn*, a piece of clothing associated in Antiquity with a *verus vir*, signify his appropriate masculinity or is it another element through which Mark renders his masculinity subversive?

Glenys Davies writes of the toga, 'what makes the garment *virilis* [manly] is not so much the toga itself as how it is worn, and the behaviour of the wearer.'[5] The *neaniskos* is wearing a delicate garment which may indicates some signs of effeminacy. Mark informs us that *sindōn* was made of linen. This detail has caused some biblical scholars to infer, due to the expensiveness of the light, soft material, that the *neaniskos* was most likely from a wealthy family.[6] But this detail is more interesting with regard to the question of masculinity, because fabric, colour, cut, and ways of wearing clothes are all part of the construction of masculinity. Lighter fabrics for the tunic and toga than wool were known and often denounced as effeminate, despite the fact that they also demonstrated the wearer's wealth. For Juvenal, wearing light garments, or being clothed in transparency, is the mark of unmanly men. This trend in senatorial fashion is in his eyes a dangerous contagion which will lead to effeminacy and cross-dressing (Juvenal, *Perluces* 2.78). Thus, for a beautiful *neaniskos* to wear a light and transparent *sindōn* during this night of terror demonstrates his unmanly behaviour.

The Roman rhetorician Quintilian provides us with powerful examples of how the way clothes are worn, and which ones, construct a man's masculinity:

'With regard to dress, there is no special garb peculiar to the orator, but his dress comes more under the public eye than that of other men. It should, therefore, be distinguished and manly, as, indeed, it ought to be with all men of position. For excessive care with regard to the cut of the toga, the style of the shoes, or the arrangement of the hair, is just as reprehensible as excessive carelessness'.
(Quintilian, *Institutio oratorio* 11.3.137–149)

So far there is nothing 'distinguished and manly' in the way that the *neaniskos*' is wearing his garment. The *neaniskos*, because of the problematics of his age, must master the art of combining and performing extraordinarily well body, dress and gesture, if he wants to be treated like a *verus vir*. Yet Mark's representation of the young man's clothes, and his way of wearing them, suggest that they fail to signify 'normal' masculinity.

IV I have nothing to wear

Not only is the young man's performance of masculinity threatened by his age and his dress, but Mark also depicts him as losing his clothes and thus even this precarious hold on a normative performance of masculinity. For ancient Jews, male nakedness meant exposure of the penis, and it was considered an offense before God.[7] We are misled if we assume that Greco-Roman culture was more liberal regarding male nudity – quite the contrary. Some philosophers described the body as 'clothing' (Seneca the Younger, *Ad Lucilium Epistulae Morales*, 66.3; Epictetus, The Discourse, 1.25.21; Marcus Aurelius, *The Meditations*, 10.1) so that death was unclothing (Philo, *Allegorical Interpretation*, 2.56.). In addition, 'nakedness was associated in the ancient Mediterranean with poverty, death, defeat, and pollution.'[8] Public nakedness could cause shame (as in Juvenal, Satires, 1.71; Plutarch, *Roman Questions*, 40; Plutarch, *Moralia*, 274A), even in the public bath, which was one of the rare sites in which the elite body was disrobed and thus the vulnerability of being penetrated was a constant threat.[9] There was never a guarantee that somebody's eyes would not de-soul one's naked body: Tacitus tells us that Emperor Tiberius denounced Piso for displaying Germanicus's naked corpse to the public for the crowd to 'handle' or 'violate with their eyes' (*Annales*, 3.12). 'Toxic shaming occurred any time, any instant, when one sensed that there was not inhibition in the eye of others, when the eyes of others would violate and consume.'[10] Thus, for Greco-Roman culture the exposure of the male naked body was both an occasion for shame and an invitation to be emasculated by the gaze of others.

In my book *Abject Bodies in the Gospel of Mark*,[11] I demonstrated how the Romans believed that there was force and power in the act of gazing. In this culture, the one who gazes emerged as an active subject and the one who is gazed upon, becomes a passive object. In this struggle of power, a manly man could 'penetrate' another body without actually possessing it. The man who was gazed upon felt penetrated by the gaze; even though his body was physically intact, he could feel dispossessed of his masculinity, degraded and humiliated for being treated like a 'woman'.

If a 'manlier eye' could violate and consume a naked male body in antiquity, we can understand the uneasiness of some biblical scholars regarding the *neaniskos*'s public nudity. Some scholars, for instance Adela Yarbo Collins, clothe the naked body of the *neaniskos* too soon when affirming: 'the young man would be wearing a light, upper garment over his underwear.'[12] According to Donahue and Harrington, this happens in order to render less problematic the young man's non-normative nakedness: 'Some argue that the young man had some clothing on underneath the *sindōn* (underwear), though that suggestion seems only to be softening the shame that the young man will experience.' Robert J. Myles also sharply criticizes those who rush to dress the *neaniskos*'s shameful naked body: 'Yet we seem blinded from recognizing such insults because the youth's nakedness gets covered up by safer scholarly discourses about eye-witness verification, angels, and ambiguous symbols for discipleship. The reign of homophobia and heteronormativity implicit within our hermeneutical filters inhibits the many possibilities of meaning-making with the biblical text.' But Mark emphasizes the *neaniskos*'s naked body and describes him as fleeing totally naked into the darkness of the night. Thus, we should avoid the temptation to clothe him only to fit social norms.

Mark accentuates the *neaniskos*'s naked body when he writes that he wears a soft linen cloth *epi gymnou* (literally, 'over naked'), and then tells us that he fled naked. As Gundry correctly puts it: 'Because the linen cloth was on his naked body, the young man fled stark naked when leaving the linen cloth in the clutches of his would-be captors.'[15] I have shown elsewhere[16] how Mark exposed Jesus's naked body to be gazed upon which subordinated Jesus not just to the power of the soldiers, but also to other 'manlier' men who look at his nakedness. Here, Mark seems to do the same with the *neaniskos*. We are invited to look upon this naked body which is fully exposed to the 'razor sharp eyes'[17] of the manlier soldiers, and is exposed, passively and vulnerably, for our own (dis)pleasure.

It has become the accepted view that a certain group of *viri militaris* existed among the legates who governed the consular military provinces in the Roman Empire. Yet in order to become these honourable manly men, the soldiers must know how to use the sword in the battlefield, and fight until death with courage. In one of Plato's dialogue we read of Socrates asking his friend Laches the 'manly' question: 'Try then if you can tell me, Laches, what courage is', and Laches responds: 'Whoever keeps his place in the rank, repels the enemy, and does not run away, is a courageous man' (*Laches*, 190E). Thus, the *neaniskos*, surrounded by the night and running naked among the 'manlier soldier', is a vulnerable body. As I argue above, clothing is inextricably linked with one's personality: 'it has the body's general shape, and it acts in many ways as a second skin, a protective barrier impervious to pain, like hair or toenails, a helpful reinforcement of the body's boundaries.'[18] In the ancient world, clothing could raise or reduce someone's personality or status. Mark's description of the young man as running away makes him appear vulnerable and renders his naked body desirable and available to be penetrated by 'the razor sharp eyes' of the soldiers.

The *neaniskos*'s nakedness in Mark anticipates the shameful death that Jesus is going to suffer by the hands of the manlier soldiers. Both the *neaniskos*'s and Jesus's nakedness show their vulnerability and precariousness as no-bodies. The *neaniskos*'s nakedness and Jesus's naked and crucified body enter into an ethical bond of unmanliness, shame, and pollution. Through this parallel, Mark's Jesus debunks heteronormative discipleship so that the impure, the poor, the sick, and the effeminate could follow Jesus.

V Run away if you want to survive!
In Greco-Roman culture, bodily movements were systematically scrutinized for signs of effeminacy. Cicero, for instance, disapproved Caesar's way of wearing a toga and walking as effeminate: 'Caesar used to belt his toga in such a way that an edge dragged and his walk looked effeminate.'[19] Ancient cloaks and mantles like our *neaniskos*'s *sindōn* '[are] likely to have been, [...] simple (i.e. sleeveless) rectangles of cloth, and they were regularly wrapped or draped around the body without any belt or fasteners of any kind to hold them on; even in the best of circumstances, consequently, they were likely to slip off with the normal movements of the body. With any sudden violent action, particularly any involving the arms or legs, the garment was practically assured of being thrown off.'[20]

Classical scholars remind us that in the Greco-Roman world '"[u]nbeltedness" is near to being the exact opposite of masculinity [...] the absence of cincture indicates defiance of convention and also unreadiness for action, in particular the inability to wear a weapon.'[21] The *neaniskos* wears his *sindōn* in what would be seen as an 'unmanly' way in this context, without a belt or sword, and thus his clothing is incapable of proving and defending his masculinity. 'In the Roman world, however, a sword is never "just" a sword: penetration invokes the opposition between conqueror and conquered, domination and submission, masculine and feminine.'[22] The sword functioned similarly to the US Marines' creed: 'This is my rifle! This is my gun [penis]! This is for fighting! This is for fun!' And not enough that the young man is displaying a lack of masculinity in his dress and comportment, he also runs rather than facing Jesus's captors and thus shows a problematic lack of aggression. 'Rather than being in the nude to engage in a "manly" contest like those who do so in gymnasia, this nameless nude dude runs away from a fight.'[23]

Bodily movements are not only an expression of our individual personality and uniqueness but are shaped by our social context. Thus, the way in which a person walks can be understood as an expression of how they perform gender norms. According to Cicero, the *veri viri*'s walk should be fast, yet not too fast, with a broad stride, bold yet not showy (Cicero, *For Sestius*, 17, 19). Their gait should still appear 'natural' and unstudied, however; feigning a way of walking could lead to the discovery of one's hidden nature, especially if that nature was effeminate (Cicero, *Against Piso*. 18). As Mark describes it, our *neaniskos*'s way of walking cannot be taken as a reflection of his masculinity because (as we stated above) he did not repels the soldiers, but rather run away in order to safe his life: '[c]apping the account of the arrest, the motif's vivid picture of abject terror and shameful nudity in cowardly flight admirably reinforces a scene in which the ruling emotion is the desperate impulse to save one's own skin, the mood of "Every man for himself."'[24] Ironically, Jesus's disciples must learn to take the cost of their 'effeminate', non-normative discipleship 'like a man', staying with Jesus during his dark night rather than running in what appears to be, on the background of Greco-Roman culture, a womanish way.

VI What does a transgressor of masculinity do in Jesus's movement?

We do not know who this 'dubious' young man is, who cowardly runs away during the shady night. However, we cannot deny that Mark underlines in his text the close relationship between this weak young and beautiful *neaniskos* and Jesus. Mark tells us that he 'was following (*synakolouthein*) Jesus'. The compound verb *synakolouthein* appears twice in Mark (5.37; 14.51) and in both instances refers to actions of disciples. Hatton argues that this verb emphasizes closeness: 'It means to accompany, to be close to, the one being followed.'[25] I stated above how this transgressor of masculinity shared the same destiny as Jesus, who died dishonoured and naked on the cross. Furthermore, Mark 14.51 tells us that soldiers tried to 'seize' the unmanful *neaniskos*, using the same verb as for Jesus's arrest (14.1.4.46.49). Thus, the *neaniskos* shared the same shameful experience of Jesus. However, in the end, he failed Jesus in the same way as the other disciples did. Therefore, it is safe to conclude that Jesus's movement included an unmanly young man who did not know how to take his faith and discipleship 'like a man'.

The close relationship between Jesus and the young man is sealed via the *sindōn*. This ambivalent piece of clothing connects the *neaniskos* with Jesus at his burial. In Mark 15.46, Jesus's dead body is clothed with a *sindōn* by Joseph of Arimathia. Thus, the *neaniskos*'s *sindōn* announces Jesus's tragic destiny. Both *neaniskos* and Jesus will suffer submission under the power of the manlier soldiers. Both bodies disappear from the narrative – one flees into the mystery of the night, and the other is laid down in the tomb. In the end, we are just left with the enigmatic *sindōn* which may reveal that God after all is not with the powerful, or '*veri viri*', but rather sides with those non-normative bodies that are deemed less than human or not human at all in a culture shaped by toxic masculinity.

VII Conclusion: What may be the implication of the *neaniskos* for us today?

In this brief passage, Mark constructs the figure of the *neaniskos* as a man who fails to live up to the standards of masculinity of his time through his vulnerable age, his luxurious clothes and exposable nakedness, his movement and behaviour. Mark's text thus 'troubles' the expectations and norms of his culture, and maybe ours, as well.

Mark presents a non-normative character of masculinity in an intimate relationship with Jesus. The author connects both characters by exposing their 'shameful' bodies for our (dis)pleasure. This unusual relationship between two broken and penetrable naked bodies is stressed via the soft *sindōn*. Thus, Mark's Jesus challenges the toxic masculinity that separates the brave from the coward, the powerful from the submissive one, the *verus vir* from the *effeminatus*. By accepting a *neaniskos* in Jesus's movement, in Mark, a new way of being 'man' and 'disciple' emerges, where service to God's kingdom has priority over other socially constructed categories such as masculinity. In Mark's gospel, discipleship means to leave one's 'normal' life and embrace the margins as a way to enter into God's kingdom. Can someone be more marginal or liminal than the *neaniskos* who has undone his masculinity in order to follow Jesus? If Jesus accepted this effeminate disciple in his community, it is time for us to remove our prejudice, homophobia, and toxic ideas of masculinity in order to celebrate Jesus's inclusive and alternative community. In the end, it is not being a 'man', 'woman', 'masculine', 'feminine', 'straight', or 'gay' that counts in discipleship. Rather, it is the willingness and generosity 'to leave everything behind' in order to announce to all Jesus's love and compassion.

Notes

1. Manuel Villalobos Mendoza, *When Men Were Not Men: Masculinity and Otherness in the Pastoral Epistles*, Sheffield: Sheffield Phoenix Press, 2014, p. 12.
2. Craig A. Williams, *Roman Homosexuality: Ideologies of Masculinity in Classical Antiquity*, New York: Oxford University Press, 2010, p. 180.
3. Jonathan Walters, 'Invading the Roman Body: Manliness and Impenetrability in Roman Thought', in Judith P. Hallett and Marilyn B. Skinner (eds.), *Roman Sexualities*, Princeton: Princeton University Press, 1997, p. 32.
4. John R. Donahue and Daniel J. Harrington, *The Gospel of Mark*, Collegeville: The Liturgical Press, 2002, p. 417.
5. Glenys Davies, 'What Made the Roman Toga *virilis*?', in Liza Cleland, Mary Harlow and Lloyd Llewellyn-Jones (eds) *The Clothed Body in the Ancient World*, Oxford: Oxbow Books, 2005, p. 121.
6. William L. Lane, *The Gospel According to Mark: The English Text with Introduction, Exposition, and Notes*, Grand Rapids: Eerdmans, 1974, p. 527.
7. Michael L. Satlow, 'Jewish Constructions of Nakedness in Late Antiquity', *Journal of Biblical Literature*, 116.3 (1997), 431.
8. Erin Vearncombes, 'Cloaks, Conflict, and Mark 14:51-52', *The Catholic Biblical Quarterly*, 75.4 (2013), 693.
9. Shadi Bartsch, *The Mirror of the Self: Sexuality, Self Knowledge, and the Gaze in the Early Roman Empire*, Chicago: University of Chicago Press, 2006, p. 159.
10. Carlin Barton, 'Being in the Eyes. Shame and Sight in Ancient Rome', in David Fredrick (ed.), *The Roman Gaze: Vision, Power, and the Body*, Baltimore: Johns Hopkins University Press, 2002, p. 223.
11. Manuel Villalobos Mendoza, *Abject Bodies in the Gospel of Mark*, Sheffield: Sheffield Phoenix Press, 2012, p. 127.
12. Adela Yarbro Collins, *Mark: A Commentary*, Minneapolis: Fortress, 2007, p. 688.
13. Donahue and Harrington, *The Gospel of Mark*, p. 417.
14. Robert J. Myles, 'Dandy Discipleship: A Queering of Mark's Male Disciples', *Journal of Men, Masculinities and Spirituality*, 4.2 (2010), 77.
15. Robert H. Gundry, *Mark: A Commentary on His Apology for the Cross*, Grand Rapids: Eerdmans, 1993, p. 882.
16. Villalobos, *Abject Bodies*, p.146.
17. Barton, 'Being in the Eyes', p. 225.
18. Nicole Wilkinson-Duran, *The Power of Disorder: Ritual Elements in Mark's Passion Narrative*, London: T. & T. Clark, 2008, p. 92.

19. Quoted in Kelly Olson, *Masculinity and Dress in Roman Antiquity*, New York: Routledge, 2017, p.144.

20. Howard M. Jackson, 'Why the Youth Shed His Cloak and Fled Naked: The Meaning and Purpose of Mark 14:51-52', *Journal of Biblical Literature*, 116 (1997), p. 280.

21. Margaret Graver, 'The Manhandling of Maecenas: Senecan Abstractions of Masculinity', *American Journal of Philology*, 119. 4 (1998), p. 620.

22. Chris Frilingos, 'Sexing the Lamb', in Stephen D. Moore and Janice C. Anderson (eds.), *New Testament Masculinities*, Atlanta: Society of Biblical Literature, 2003, p. 316.

23. Tat-siong Benny Liew, 'Re-Mark-able Masculinities: Jesus, the Son of Man, and the (Sad) Sum of Manhood?', in Stephen D. Moore and Janice C. Anderson (eds.), *New Testament Masculinities*, Atlanta: Society of Biblical Literature, 2003, p.115.

24. Jackson, 'Why the Youth Shed His Cloak', 286.

25. Stephen B. Hatton, 'Mark's Naked Disciple: The Semiotic and Comedy of Following', *Neotestamentica*, 35.1/2 (2001), 37.

Masculinities, Religion, and Sexualities

EZRA CHITANDO

Religion continues to be a significant factor in the shaping and performance of masculinities and sexualities in different parts of the world. This article explores how religion influences masculinities and sexualities in general, utilizing some examples from the African context. While highlighting that masculinities occur in the plural, it also underscores the contestations around sexualities. The article probes how religion influences straight, gay and celibate sexualities. It also draws attention to strategic areas that could facilitate the emergence of more liberative masculinities and sexualities.

I Introduction

There is a growing interest in the field of masculinities globally. In order to highlight the dynamics around masculinities, religion and sexualities, this article utilizes the African context. Masculinities globally and in Africa have come under serious contestation. The forces, spheres and modes of contestation are as multiple as they are intense. These pressures are due to rapid social change where notions of men as 'bread winners' have been exploded, the assertive African women's movement, the impact of missionary religions such as Christianity and Islam, as well as the effectively organized lesbian, gay, bisexual, transgender and intersex (LGBTI) movement and others. African Traditional Religions have also been undergoing rapid transformation as they adjust to changing social realities. Whereas the earlier assumptions around masculinity were built on heteronormativity and tended to gloss over internal differences, it is becoming increasingly clear that there are diverse ways of expressing one's maleness. Therefore, there is a clear turn towards appreciating that there are masculinities in the plural, including in Africa.[1] There is a growing realization that masculinities are definitely not uniform and that they are expressed in diverse and sometimes conflicting ways.

This article seeks to highlight the interpenetration among religion, masculinities and sexualities. In the first section, the article outlines the major themes in the study of masculinities. The second section discusses the interplay among Christianity, masculinities and sexualities. It has three parts that focus on straight, gay and celibate sexualities. The third section highlights some of the strategic areas that can assist in promoting transformative masculinities and sexualities.

II Major themes in the study of masculinities
A longer narrative is required to do justice to the complexity of masculinities in global scholarship.[2] In this section, I seek to summarize the key issues in contemporary masculinities, illustrating them with examples from Africa (bearing in mind the reality that Africa is a vast continent characterized by radical pluralism). Thus, the dimensions associated with masculinities in Africa can be regarded as a useful indicator of the debates at the global level. To say this, however, is not to deny that masculinities in Africa have their own unique, but not exotic, characteristics. To begin with, there is an appreciation of the co-existence of 'traditional' and 'modern' masculinities in Africa. These categories are by no means stable, as they continue to shift over time. For example, in their analysis of black (African) transnational masculinities, Dominic Pasura and Anastasia Christou highlight how the new setting in London challenges expectations associated with masculinity on the continent.[3] As the African case study illustrates, masculinities are constantly being worked and reworked, refusing to be fixed.

One of the most topical issues in masculinities relates to their relationship with violence. Globally, there is an interest in understanding how masculinities are implicated in violence in general, including mass violence. Further, activists have drawn attention to the interface between masculinities and sexual and gender-based violence. Some men's groups dedicated to campaigns against sexual and gender-based violence, such as the White Ribbon Campaign, have utilized insights from such studies.

Although studies on masculinities and violence (including sexual and gender-based violence) are very informative, they do run the risk of writing off an entire gender as violent and retrogressive.

Alongside the focus on masculinities and violence, there is a growing emphasis on youth masculinities. The insight from feminist studies that one is born male or female, but that it is society that makes one a man or a woman, has drawn attention to the power of socialization in the construction of gender. Further, as Judith Butler has argued, persuasively in my opinion, 'biological' sex too is a social construction.[4] Consequently, there has been an interest in how adolescent boys and young men understand and express their masculinities. Given the fact that there are many more young people than adults in Africa, there has been an investment in exploring the interface between young men and the construction of masculinity.[5]

The role of religion in shaping masculinities has begun receiving due attention. The upsurge in the role of religion globally has discredited the secularization thesis, namely, the idea that as human societies attain high levels of economic development, religion would become less important and even disappear, and thus, religion has become a central concept in the humanities and social sciences yet again. In Africa in particular, scholars have been keen to identify the impact of African Traditional Religions, Christianity, and Islam in shaping masculinities.[6]

Consistent with the growing focus on religion and masculinities is the emergence of a sub-discipline that has been called, 'critical men's studies in religion'. It is located within the larger academic study of religion but has the goal of isolating masculinity as a category of analysis for in-depth scrutiny. Whereas gender in religious studies has been largely associated with 'women's studies', the study of religion, men, and masculinities endeavours to recover the original meaning of gender as socially constructed roles of women and men in society. Björn Krondorfer, one of the prime movers of the discipline, writes:

'A "critical men's studies in religion" approach is part of this larger mode of discernment; it asks questions specifically pertaining to men and masculinities in the religious traditions, querying and critiquing men's identities and performances as well as assumed male authority and power. It can also include questions about male-gendered imaginings of the divine.'[7]

Scholars within this field have been keen to identify the role of religions in promoting male dominance in society. They have also explored the patriarchal assumptions behind most of the world's religions, alongside exploring how this has led to the exclusion of women from leadership in religious communities and society at large. In the context of African religious leadership, scholars have examined how notions of headship, appeals to sacred texts, and the ideological deployment of culture and tradition have been used to justify gender-based violence by men, as well as men's leadership of institutions.[8] Consequently, activists have called for more liberative approaches where religion can and must promote more life-giving masculinities. For example, the Circle of Concerned African Women Theologians, one of the most consistent groupings of academics dedicated to gender justice, has been insistent that religions must give birth to more progressive masculinities.[9]

III Contested frontiers: Religions, masculinities and sexualities

Emerging within the study of religions and masculinities is the focus on sexualities. Intriguingly, although religions have had a lot to say about sexuality (through their tendency to try and police it), reflections on religions, masculinities and sexualities in Africa have not been as consistent as one would have expected. Apart from African women theologians, most African scholars of religion and theology have not been as forthcoming in addressing religions and sexuality in the three main religions of Africa, namely, African Traditional Religions, Islam, and Christianity. Nonetheless, there is an emerging interest in this theme, with various scholars analysing how religions (or certain versions, interpretations, or expressions of them) both prescribe and proscribe particular sexualities. For example, most versions of African Traditional Religions, Christianity, and Islam have been interpreted and deployed as promoting heteronormativity and as condemning homosexuality. However, closer readings of their sacred texts and traditions, such as the story of Sodom and Gomorrah in Genesis 19, 'queer' these texts, that is, facilitate newer and redemptive interpretations. Three scholars active in this field in Africa have maintained that the passage, which has been a 'text of terror' for homosexuals in the world, must be reinterpreted. Thus:

'Rereading the toxic so-called homosexuality texts demythologises them and enables queer Christianity to talk back to the Christian establishment [...] Rereading these texts also offers other more redemptive interpretive options. For example, if Genesis 18–19 "really" is about hospitality and not homosexuality, then perhaps this text can be read for inclusion of and hospitality towards "strange(r)" sexualities. At the very least, the text speaks to the role of protecting the stranger from the established culture of the time. Just as Abram (and later Lot) defended the stranger from abuse, he also negotiated the protection of the people of Sodom and Gomorrah.'[10]

The role of religions in shaping masculinities and the imagined sexualities that must go with it has resulted in contradictions and hypocrisy. For example, Christianity has generally upheld an ethic of abstaining from sex before marriage and mutual fidelity in marriage. This model is often presented simplistically and is built on the assumption of heteronormativity. An ideal scheme is formulated where the adolescent boy who grows into a young man abstains from sex until he is married to his virgin female partner. Alternatively, if he takes up the vow of celibacy, as in some faith traditions, he remains celibate for the rest of his life. Such a model of the 'faithful husband', many proponents proclaim, is the surest way of addressing sexually transmitted infections and HIV. The discourse on sex and sexuality in such religious settings is guided by 'old time religion' and seeks to nurture masculinities that encourage men to get on the straight path, and retain them on this path. However, this focus on personal morality overlooks the reality that vulnerability to HIV is due to complex systemic factors, and not simply one's sexual behaviour.

However, it has become clear that the conservative religious approach to masculinities and sexuality faces a number of challenges. In particular, the tendency to demonize the body in Christianity is counterproductive. The fear of the masculine body's potency (alongside the notion of the 'dangerous' female body) has led to three main challenges. To begin with, the ideology of 'puritanical' masculinities that are undergirded by religion (especially Christianity) has come under increasing scrutiny. For example, some young men are questioning the insistence on abstinence, calling upon religious leaders to be more flexible in their teachings on sexualities.

However, there are also some who acknowledge these teachings and strive to uphold them in their own lives, leading to conflicting positions regarding the value of pre-marital sexuality for young men.[11] Thus, there is tension over the practicability of the Christian teachings on sexualities. Secondly, there is contestation over the assumption that religions can only approve heterosexuality. The LGBTI movement has emerged as a significant player in different parts of the world and has challenged the faith communities to review their stance on homosexuality. Third, there has been a shift in both academia and activism to promote sex-positive theologies. That is, religions are called to regard sexuality more positively and to have more confidence in the body. In the context of Africa, initiatives such as the International Network of Religious Leaders Living with and Personally Affected by HIV and AIDS (INERELA), and the World Council of Churches (WCC) Ecumenical HIV and AIDS Initiatives and Advocacy (EHAIA) have been actively involved in the struggle to encourage faith communities to embrace the body, as well as sex and sexuality, as being integral to what it means to be human.

(a) Religions, masculinities, and straight sexualities

Across cultures, religions have tended to promote masculinities that prioritize straight sexualities. Hegemonic masculinities in most societies are buttressed by religious myths that present the able-bodied, straight man as a 'real man'. In this scheme, all other sexualities, particularly homosexuality, become inferior and are ranked below straight sexualities. Sacred texts, inherited beliefs, and traditions are all marshalled to promote and protect straight sexualities. Regrettably, this often generates homophobia.[12]

Religious ideologies serve to prop up straight sexualities and to police all other sexualities. Thus, there is a complex and dynamic play amongst the concepts of religion, masculinities and sexualities. Religions frame masculinities, which in turn find expression and affirmation in sexualities. Sexualities are crucial, therefore, to the imagination and expression of masculinities. The notion of a 'real man' is bound up with assumptions about his (supposed) straight sexuality. In the religious (and patriarchal) ideology, anything else is a contradiction in terms. It is not surprising that straight sexualities are prioritized and projected as having been granted

56

the 'divine seal of approval' across many religions and cultures.

To be fair, religions also seek to control straight sexualities and to promote 'responsible masculinities'. Thus, we find an emphasis on self-control, faithfulness in relationships and nurturing loving, monogamous (or, in the case of Islam, the option of closed polygamous) marriages in religious teachings on straight sexuality. In addition, in the context of Africa (but also elsewhere), straight sexualities are associated with the capacity to reproduce. Although there are other factors that are integral to constituting masculinities, sexuality is a key component. Thus:

> 'Sex is only one of several thematic factors that resource the dominant masculinity narrative, but it is without doubt a significant one. Nearly everywhere in the world manliness is closely associated with our sexual partner(s), the sexual appeal of our partner(s), the size of our penises, the claims we make about our sexual stamina, whether we can maintain a healthy erection and how virile we are.'[13]

Straight masculinities and sexualities have, however, come under severe stress in the contemporary period. The 'sacred canopy' under which they have historically thrived has been challenged. Further, the idea that straight masculinities grant straight men the right to dominate women, children, and other men has been rendered problematic due to contestations within straight masculinities themselves. The assumed homogeneity of straight masculinities has been exposed by the fault lines that follow the cleavages of race, age, class, region, religion, and others. In Africa, as elsewhere, rapid social change has brought with it the 'burden of masculinity', and straight sexualities are buckling under its strain. The contradictions of straight sexualities, particularly the challenge of living up to the ideals of sexual prowess while at the same time being restrained by ideals of self-control and – in some religions – abstinence, have become all too clear. Thus, straight sexualities promoted by the three main religions of Africa have fundamental flaws and need to adopt a more realistic perspective.

(b) Religions, masculinities, and gay sexualities

Religions have generally not brought good news to non-normative masculinities and sexualities in Africa, and globally. Whereas there has been some progress in acknowledging and embracing gay sexualities in different parts of the world, it remains clear, as discussed above, that straight sexualities have found much greater acceptance in comparison to all other sexualities. Consequently, gay sexualities continue to struggle for a place in the sun, as religious and cultural ideologies have formed powerful covenants to oppress them. Religions have often cast non-normative masculinities and sexualities as innately sinful and unacceptable. In the context of Africa, some politicians have used attacks on gay sexualities as a ploy to gain mileage with religious communities. They have sought to appeal to followers of African Traditional Religions, Christianity, and Islam by demonizing gay sexualities. Instead of investing in tackling the pressing problems of (and with) their citizens, they have spent time attacking gay sexualities. This diversion has the effect of projecting such politicians as God-fearing, thereby attracting support from adherents of the different religions who happen to espouse mainly conservative theologies.

Gay sexualities have been constructed as occupying a rung lower than straight sexualities. The same religio-cultural ideology portrays gay sexualities as effeminate and as betraying 'real masculinity'. In this scheme, gay masculinity is policed and threatened for not defending masculine honour (which is associated with straight sexuality). Conservative versions of different religions attack gay sexualities for allegedly frustrating the divine plan of clearly defined genders and the complementary relationships between distinct male and female beings. In addition, since gay sexuality is not associated with procreation directly, it is subject to constant attacks by conservative religious actors.

Religious opposition to gay sexuality also stems from the imagined ideal of a compact and stable nuclear family. This ideal has gained ground in post-colonial African contexts and has begun to undercut the cherished notion of the extended family. In fact, some versions of African Pentecostalism associate the extended family with the cult of the ancestors and discourage fraternizing with relatives in the larger community. Thus, part of the contestation over gay sexuality and the discourse over 'family values' is based in the idea that there (must) subsist everywhere and at all times families made up of a man and a woman, children and pets living happily ever after. The argument is that gay sexuality threatens this tantalizing ideal by setting up the idea or possibility of a different family. This is notwithstanding the fact that although the nuclear family is much cherished, throughout history and in the contemporary period, other types of families have always existed. There will almost always be more non-nuclear families than nuclear families in any society at any given point in time.

Gay sexuality has been negotiating with, resisting and even dismissing religious traditions as it strives for acceptance in society. In those places where religions have a much greater presence and say in public life, such as in Africa, gay sexuality continues to experience greater levels of discomfort. However, there has been notable progress, with some religious leaders openly expressing the view that their religions are not intrinsically homophobic. Further, some scholars have highlighted how some religions have either not criticized, or have embraced, homosexuality.[14] Utilizing liberative dimensions within the different religions, the LGBTI movement and its allies are making some commendable progress in Africa and other parts of the world. The progress can be seen in the extent to which sexual diversity has been forced onto the agenda, particularly in discourses on HIV and AIDS. Further, the scrapping of colonial pieces of legislation that prohibited same-sex sexual relations in a number of African countries highlights such progress. Such developments would have been unthinkable about a decade ago.

(c) Religions, masculinities, and celibate sexuality
Celibate sexuality occupies a complex place in the ranking of masculinities by religions. On the one hand, the celibate and childless man is celebrated for his ability to master the body and its demands, while on the other hand his masculinity can be questioned on exactly the same grounds. This is particularly the case in Christianity. Thus, celibate sexuality is often characterized by ambivalence in religious contexts. However, in Africa the concept has come under sustained attack due to the association between masculinity and virility. The African traditional understanding of masculinity has been that a man is supposed to invest in perpetuating the lineage particularly through male progeny, and thus celibacy is considered

'un-manly' and problematic.

Two additional issues need to be highlighted. First, the framing of celibacy as a reflection of masculine discipline and conquest of the flesh emerges from Christian theologies that find the body problematic, as already mentioned above. Thus, celibacy is taken to represent the ultimate masculine achievement, namely, gaining complete control of the body's desire for sex (although sexuality transcends sex). Second, there is a danger that celibacy can play the same role as machismo, that is, detesting femininity in all its forms and promoting either masculine distance from or conquest of femininity. However, the practice or ideal of celibacy is limited to versions of Christianity and is not actively promoted in African Traditional Religions and Islam.

IV Religions, masculinities, and sexualities: Ongoing sites of opportunity

The interplay among religions, masculinities, and sexualities brings up a very queer picture indeed. It is a messy and complex interaction. In this section, I seek to highlight some of the strategic areas for the (possible) transformation of masculinities within the faith sector. In turn, this would facilitate the recognition of liberative (as opposed to oppressive) sexualities. Although I draw attention to these areas with special reference to the African context, I am convinced that they have resonance in other parts of the world.

Engaging with conservative theologies and interpretations of gender, masculinities, and sexualities

The appeal of an invented and idealized 'old time religion' is difficult to dispel. Religious people have historically thrived on the understanding that there are certain and fixed dogmas that do not change. Thus, conservative interpretations of the identity and roles of men as decreed by God/the Sacred will continue to appeal to many believers. In Africa, this has seen debates on masculinities, sexualities, and access to sexual and reproductive health, rights, and services being dominated by those who swear by their sacred texts. Consequently, scholars and activists who wish to see a world characterized by gender justice must budget for resistance from this particular sector. To say this, however, is not to suggest that religions are always opposed to the quest for gender justice. Indeed, when sound strategies are employed, religions can become effective allies or even provide the setting/context in the quest for gender justice.

Need for life-giving and progressive readings of sacred texts to promote transformative masculinities and sexualities

Sacred texts and traditions provide believers with guides to belief and action. They are very significant in shaping attitudes towards diverse masculinities and femininities. For example, in Africa, the Bible and the Qur'an are the two texts that are central to the lives of many communities. In many instances, they will be accorded more authority than the national constitution(s). Therefore, while the progress in removing sections that criminalized homosexuality from the statute books in some African countries such as Mozambique and Angola is noteworthy, and the recent legal triumph of LGBTI organizations in Botswana is notable, more needs to be done. Creative and progressive interpretations of the sacred texts to promote transformative masculinities are required in order to change attitudes. Placing emphasis on Africa's own struggle for the rights and dignity of all, recovering texts that celebrate sexualities, and highlighting the message of tolerance within the sacred texts is quite effective.

Acknowledging the influence of femininities in shaping masculinities and sexualities

Perhaps the study of masculinities and the accompanying sexualities has tended to shift towards the extreme of exclusivism. There is need to acknowledge that femininities have a major role in shaping masculinities. The tensions that are emerging from men who have embraced non-aggressive masculinities meeting resistance from women who are guarding roles and spaces that have traditionally been associated with women and femininities serve as a timely reminder that both forms of gender expression need to be transformed *simultaneously*. Although femininities are often placed in opposition to masculinities, in reality masculinities are always in dialogue and negotiation with femininities. Therefore, it is important for scholars and activists to continue to analyse the two *together*.

V Conclusion

Far from being a relic, religion continues to have a significant say in the formation and expression of masculinities and sexualities. Religious ideologies, and interpretations of sacred texts and traditions, contribute to the imagining and performance of masculinities (and femininities) and sexualities. Whereas the dominant paradigm has been for religions to insist on specific versions of masculinity and to privilege straight sexuality, ongoing contestations have brought about new realities. They have made us see that religious traditions are not quite as clear-cut in their ideas of masculinity and sexuality as we have often assumed. In particular, gay sexualities have become more assertive and have challenged conservative interpretations of gender and sexualities. If the study of religion is to continue to contribute towards generating humanistic knowledge, it must invest more in exploring how religions can generate and nurture more life-giving masculinities and sexualities.

Notes

1. See for example, Lahoucine Ouzgane and Robert Morrell (eds.), *African Masculinities: Men in Africa from the Late Nineteenth Century to the Present*, New York: Palgrave Macmillan, 2005.
2. See the contribution by Raewyn Connell in this volume.
3. Dominic Pasura and Anastasia Christou, 'Theorizing Black (African) Transnational Masculinities', *Men and Masculinities*, 21.4 (2018), 521–546.
4. Judith Butler, 'Performative Acts and Gender Constitution: An Essay in Phenomenology and Feminist Theory', *Theatre Journal*, 40.4 (1988), 519–531.
5. See for example: Gary Barker and Christine Ricardo, 'Young Men and the Construction of Masculinity in Sub-Saharan Africa: Implications for HIV/AIDS, Conflict, and Violence', *Social Development Working Paper* No. 26, Washington: World Bank, 2005.
6. See for example, Ezra Chitando and Sophie Chirongoma (eds.), *Redemptive Masculinities: Men, HIV and Religion*, Geneva: World Council of Churches, 2012.
7. Björn Krondorfer, 'God's Hinder Parts and Masculinity's Troubled Fragmentations: Trajectories of Critical Men's Studies in Religion', *Preprints and Working Papers of the Centre for Religion and Modernity*, Münster, 2017, 2, at https://www.uni-muenster.de/imperia/md/content/religion_und_moderne/preprints/crm_working_paper_14_krondorfer_neu.pdf.
8. See for example, Lovemore Togarasei, 'Pauline Challenge to African Masculinities: Reading Pauline Texts in the Context of HIV/AIDS', *Acta Theologica*, Supp. 16 (2012), 148–160; Chitando and Chirongoma, *Redemptive Masculinities*; and Adriaan van Klinken, 'Male Headship as Male Agency: An Alternative Understanding of a "Patriarchal" African Pentecostal Discourse on Masculinity', *Religion and Gender*, 1.1 (2011), 104–124.

9. See for example, Zorodzai Dube, 'The African Women Theologians' Contribution towards the Discussion about Alternative Masculinities', *Verbum et Ecclesia*, 37.2 (2016), a1577, doi: 10.4102./ve.v37i2.1577.

10. Gerald West, Charlene Van der Walt and Kapya J. Kaoma, 'When Faith Does Violence: Reimagining Engagement between Churches and LGBTI Groups on Homophobia in Africa', *HTS Teologiese Studies/Theological Studies*, 72.1 (2016), a3511, doi. org/10.4102/ hts.v72i1.3511.

11. Hendrey Lusey, Miguel San Sebastian, Monica Christianson, Lars Dahlgren and Kerstin E. Edin, 'Conflicting Discourses of Church Youths on Masculinity and Sexuality in the Context of HIV in Kinshasa, Democratic Republic of Congo', *SAHARA J*, 11.1 (2014), 84–93, doi: 10.1080/17290376.2014.930695.

12. Elijah G. Ward, 'Homophobia, Hypermasculinity and the US Black Church', *Culture, Health, and Sexuality*, 7.5 (2005), 493–504.

13. Kopano Ratele, 'Male Sexualities and Masculinities', in Sylvia Tamale (ed.), *African Sexualities: A Reader*, Cape Town: Pambazuka Press, 2011, p. 399.

14. See for example, Ronald Long, *Men, Homosexuality, and the Gods: An Exploration into the Religious Significance of Male Homosexuality in World Perspective*, New York: Routledge, 2004.

Masculinity, Race, Fatherhood

VINCENT LLOYD

The harms caused by toxic forms of masculinity appear different in marginalized communities where gender is used as a tool of marginalization. This poses a particular challenge in the case of Black Americans, where both gender and kinship relations were stripped in slavery and pathologised during slavery's afterlives, making masculinity and fatherhood together particularly vexed issues. Efforts to 'redeem' masculinity, from this perspective, often sound much like white supremacist efforts to manage Black masculinity. The autobiography of executed gang leader Stanley Tookie Williams provides a particularly fruitful site for reflecting on the possibilities and limitations of redeeming Black manhood, given Williams's interest in spiritual disciplines.

I The ends of masculinity

If masculinity names a discrete set of social practices, and if we come to the realization that those social practices cause a good deal of harm, it should be straightforward to eliminate, or virtually eliminate, masculinity. This scenario portrays masculinity like cigarette smoking: once we realized cigarettes cause cancer, it was only a matter of time until smoking was wiped out of mainstream culture – over the objections of powerful corporate interests. For a time, cigarette smoking was associated with great leaders and great cultural and aesthetic achievements (for example, in Westerns), but that connection was contingent rather than necessary. Now that we realize masculinity, too, is 'toxic,' feeding violence that is physical, social, psychic, and spiritual, is it only a matter of time until masculinity is no more?

Or perhaps what we need are kinder, gentler forms of masculinity. In this view, the problem is with masculinity at its extremes, with the toxic masculinity that, as a component of the ideology of patriarchy, results in hostile work environments, sexual violence, pay inequality, and glass ceilings. Put another way, we need new answers to the question: What does it mean to be a good man? Instead of imagining masculine excellence in terms of power, self-discipline, rationality, and physical prowess, masculine excellence ought to involve rationality and emotional sensitivity, power and gentleness, self-discipline and vulnerability, strength and caring – or some such healthy balance.

Both the desire to eliminate masculinity and the desire to improve masculinity rest on an assumption that masculinity names a discrete set of social practices, but if masculinity is a component of patriarchy, and patriarchy is a deep and broad system of domination shaping our capacity to perceive the world and ourselves and so to act, a system of domination interlocking with other systems of domination including racism, colonialism, and empire, then these desires to eliminate or improve are twins, and equally misguided. The response to evidence of harms associated with masculinity ought to be attacking patriarchy, a project that requires focused analysis and organizing.

Liberation theology – and the Bible – teaches us to look toward marginalized communities for privileged normative insights, for revelations of the divine that can guide life in the world. In the contemporary United States, this means, for example, attending to questions of masculinity among Black Americans. One of the means through which marginalization is caused and confirmed is ascribing pathological gender roles to a subordinate community. Black Americans are classed as hyper-sexual and asexual, excessively masculine or feminine or deficiently masculine or feminine. Then, the superordinate community (whites) decrees that such pathological gender and sexuality must be managed (through regulation) or eliminated (through, at its extreme, castration, an essential part of lynching rituals). The impulse to find a kinder, gentler masculinity, or to eliminate masculinity altogether, appears quite different in this context: it appears complicit with the status quo, with the forces of white supremacy. It is only self-hating Blacks, Blacks entranced by the false promise that respectability will secure a place of equality in the white world, who would participate in the discourse of managing or eliminating masculinity. However, as patriarchy and white supremacy interlock, Black Americans are particularly motivated to analyse and attack patriarchy. The difference between a moralizing discourse about masculinity and the practice of analysing and attacking patriarchy is subtle but crucial.

The case of Black Americans is a particular, extreme case of marginalization, perhaps a paradigm of marginalization. The experience of enslavement strips away the possibility of kinship and ungenders.[1] The 'pathologies' of Black American kinship and gender lamented today, and in the past century and a half, are produced by slavery's afterlives. The norms, values, habits, and modes of reasoning, feeling, and imagining that made it possible to treat a Black person as a thing persisted even after the legal regime of slavery came to an end. Blacks could be parents, but they would necessarily be perceived as bad parents; they could be women, but they would necessarily fail to live up to the standards of womanhood; and so, too, for Black men and masculinity.

A recurrent theme in the most renowned writings of Black men is the desire to be fully men, and the impossibility of that desire. To be a man here has no relation to biology, nor is it exhausted by the social practices of masculinity. Rather, to be a man means to be an authority, to set rules for oneself rather than to have rules arbitrarily imposed on one. This is closely connected with the desire to have a father and to be a father, where fatherhood represents authority, possessed not only for oneself but for one's family. To be a man and to be father and to refuse domination: these three become one in the desires of Black writers, and they are triply refused to their aspirants by white supremacy. Richard Wright's *Native Son*, Ralph Ellison's *Invisible Man*, and James Baldwin's protagonist in *Go Tell It on the Mountain* each seek, in different ways, again and again, something which is foreclosed to them – to be free, to have and be a father, to be a man.

Wright, Ellison, and Baldwin describe Black narrators looking for paternity, and discovering that the role of father, as they imagined it, is foreclosed. White supremacy disrupts the pathway from the norms of an authoritative father to the norms of the world: Blackness means always being on the wrong side of worldly norms. The knot of fatherhood, authority, and masculinity does not hold: finding a father or a man is not assurance that one has found an authority. Put another way, when we look at society's margins, the privilege given to the social practices of masculinity, the way they are treated as authoritative, is unstable. This does not mean that masculinity at the margins is harmless. Those who seek authority may perform masculinity excessively, or idiosyncratically, sometimes causing grave harms (for example, in domestic violence and sexual abuse). But masculinity from the margins, in authority's shadow, also involves a dynamism that permits critical questions and novel experiments in masculinity.

II Stanley Tookie Williams as God-Father

Let us turn to one narrative that particularly dramatizes masculinity from the margins, grappling with the presumed connection between masculinity, fatherhood, and authority – and reflecting on the ideological and idolatrous forces that attempt to sanctify that triad. This is the story of and by a Black man who was killed by the state. Stanley Tookie Williams was executed on December 13, 2005. The year before, he penned an autobiography, *Blue Rage, Black Redemption*, that tracks his religious salvation alongside his salvation as a father and as a man. Writing a year before his execution, as his fame was growing, Williams thought he had triumphed: 'To poor people, prisoners, slaves, and the disenfranchised everywhere – through faith and theories put into practice, you can bend the most oppressive circumstances to your will, to make the impossible possible' (vii).[2] It garnered him a Nobel Prize nomination, but not a stay of his execution: a quite different model of masculinity, Arnold Schwarzenegger, then governor of California, ordered him killed by lethal injection.

Williams grew up after the civil rights movement, after the black power movement. There was no longer a sense that mass movements would end racial inequality. Laws of segregation had fallen, but there were still the police: 'Every child in the neighbourhood knew that cops were the enemy' (12). State institutions did not provide stable normative authority. The state's authority was wielded arbitrarily, to dominate Blacks. And there was no alternative space for Black institutions and authorities to develop. The same forces of domination that harassed Black children removed and encaged their fathers: 'Mass incarceration has become a divisive force that splits families and foments a son's resentment for his father' (319). In the moment, it felt as if individual police officers are racist, as if fathers are irresponsible. With a bird's eye view, it became clear that the system of white supremacy is denying Black authority. Whether it was police violence or imprisonment, economic deprivation or the health consequences of environmental devastation, Williams will come to recognize racial domination's effects on the bodies and lives of Black Americans.

On the surface, Williams was a man defined by fathers. He was Stanley Tookie Williams III, bearing the name of his father and grandfather. But that father had left the family before the young Williams turned one, and his grandfather experienced such economic hardship due to his race that his health deteriorated, and he died young. The young Williams is a naughty boy, getting himself in deeper and deeper trouble as he grows. Authority, for him, can only mean domination: the arbitrary violence of the police. Eventually, his mother decides to bring the young Williams to his father to straighten him out, but from the youth's perspective, his father is no different than the police officers: just another man trying to exercise his arbitrary will over the boy. 'When he decreed that I was going to school every day whether I liked it or not, I asked, "Are you man enough to make me?"' (112). Masculinity means strength and the capacity to use it to enforce one's arbitrary will, this is what the young Williams had concluded. 'I promised myself I'd never be anything like my father,' Williams reports, but on reflection, from prison, he realizes that he became exactly like his father (320).

Williams's mother attempted to impose order on the family, to teach Williams right from wrong. But her teachings had little effect, and Williams continued to get into trouble. In part, Williams explains this by the incompatibility between the set of norms imposed by his mother and the set of norms imposed by 'the street', that is, the world of boys and girls, men and women outside the home. There, self-interest and strength ruled supreme, not right and wrong. 'Might was right, always' (15). This was not an honourable street governed by noble principles. To the contrary, 'The prime rule of fighting was this: there were no rules, anything goes' (35).[3] From the perspective of the street, Williams's mother's rules seemed arbitrary as well, just one more form of domination, this one sanctioned by his mother's Christianity. She would administer 'Biblical beatings' that followed her prayers. 'That swift backhand upside my head must have been God's response', Williams concludes (42). Here God is just one among the cast of characters Williams encounters who arbitrarily exercise violence on his body.

Williams decides to escape those around him pushing systems of rules: God and school, father and mother. He embraces life on the street, but in doing so he finds himself in need of another system of rules. The street was chaotic, with small gangs fighting and stealing. He decides to make order out of this chaos, this time by authoring his own set of norms and imposing it on others. With friends he merged several small gangs into a super-gang, the Crips, governed by rules and imposing rules on street life. 'Crip was my religion. I was its co-creator and star-crossed prophet, and I critiqued all other Crips by my own standards' (242). This was a religion of vengeance. Every wrong required a violent response; there was no turning the other cheek. And it was a new family, with each member of the Crips addressing each other as cousin, 'Cuz'. Along with imposing his rules on others in the street, becoming a father figure for a generation of young, impoverished Black men in Los Angeles, Williams cultivated the image of hyper-masculinity, first and foremost by weightlifting. His muscles grew enormous together with his authority, the two entwined: 'My enormous size from pumping iron also frightened the hell out of the authorities' (219). Yet this combination was unstable. It was always ultimately responsive to and dependent on other authorities, particularly the police, and Williams reports that his efforts at establishing Crip order were always undercut by his own volatility. It was not that the Crips established an island of peace in an ocean of anti-Black tyranny; rather, the Crips established another form of tyranny, with its arbitrary violence afflicting participants themselves – a fact Williams was reminded of acutely when he was shot.

III Redeeming fatherhood, redeeming masculinity

Williams survived the bullet, but he would wind up in prison. There, the state directly assumed the role of father-substitute, of ultimate, tyrannical authority, dominating and humiliating. And it was there, at his lowest point, 'treated worse than an animal' (221), so full of prison-administered pharmaceuticals that he was 'reduced to marionette status' (226), that

Williams began to identify interlocking systems of domination as the ultimate cause of his anger. He began to realize that using his anger to fuel his own tyranny would be self-destructive. The first step was to discipline himself, this time not motivated by his passions but rather in order to form his passions. He continued weight-lifting, but now as part of a regime of practices he imposed on himself for physical and mental health, including fasting and praying. Once he had worked on self-discipline, he sets about learning other disciplines so that he can use them for his own purposes. He set about systematically improving his vocabulary so that he could use language to express himself, and he learned to draw so that he could use art to express himself. He set about learning the legal system to better defend himself in court. And he set about learning from religious and political systems circulating in prison – from Christianity to Afrocentrism, from Islam to socialism – not to choose one to embrace but to find practices from each useful for him.

Altogether, Williams gave himself a 'godlike power to create', but now, 'redeemed', this power was used for justice rather than tyranny (245). He was not redeemed in a flash, or by following a voice from the heavens, or by reading a particular book. On his account, redemption came through practice, through imposing regimes on himself and so keeping his self-interest in check. In this way, through something like spiritual disciplines, Williams reports, 'I discovered the means to control my ego, which enabled me to reunite with God; to reclaim my humanity; to discover inner peace; and to find my raison d'etre' (xix).

A prison fire caused Williams to realize that he could not just stand with incarcerated Crips. All those incarcerated were in the same boat (though not all those in prison; Williams' sense of solidarity did not extend to guards). At the same time Williams was disciplining himself, he was analysing systems of domination in the world and how they were connected. He discovered the reach of white supremacy, how it had concealed Black and African history from him and his peers, how it had destroyed his sense of self-worth. Education and introspection were among Williams's new disciplining practices, and these led to an increasingly sharp critical sensibility. Here, finally, as physical discipline and intellectual critique came into unity, Williams became a redeemed man; he came to 'develop a conscience' (301). Even then, however, redemption was incomplete. He was on the correct path now, but not at the destination. Williams describes the motivating force of his new life simply: 'Faith in God' (325). This is not a passive faith, but rather it requires action: 'I fight for the poor and wretched' (336).

Put another way, Williams learned how to become a man. He realizes that before, on the street, it was a 'Machiavellian mentality that served for years as my apologia for manhood' (269). Now, his manhood could be fulfilled as his body and mind sharpened, his emotions in harmony with his reason. Whereas before, 'fatherhood scared me' (321), and he convinced his partners not to list him on his two children's birth certificates as the father, now he relished the experience of fatherhood. In the final, climactic pages of his autobiography, Williams describes a jail-house reunion with his son, Stan. 'His resemblance to me was striking. It was like looking in a mirror' (327). Stan had followed his father into gangster life, trying to imitate his father. Williams tells Stan that he was not worthy of imitation because he did not have the courage to be a father to his sons – but now he had learned how to live rightly and to love rightly. As they parted, 'almost as one, we spoke two words: "Perfect love!"' (329). Williams reports finally feeling redeemed. Just as, with the Crips, Williams would spread his rule beyond himself and his circle of intimates, redeemed, Williams wrote a series of children's books to spread his new rule, or rather, his new understanding of the spiritual disciplines. 'I continue trying to set a noble example for my sons and others. My faith and discipline are the pillars of my resolve' (324).

Williams had sons who loved him: he had become the man he always wanted to be but thought he could never be. For Williams reports that the start of his troubles, at the end of elementary school, was when he had a medical problem that required a radical circumcision causing excruciating physical and psychic pain. From that point on, he no longer had a vision of his future, no sense that dreams he once harboured could be achieved. Life was reduced to mechanically doing what was done. Sensual desire brought with it horrendous pain. With his injured member, he could hardly engage in the world, let alone be a man – and certainly not a father. It does not take an overzealous Freudian to read Williams's life story, then, as consisting of attempts to realize his compromised manhood, first by combating apparent tyrannies around him with his own tyrannical rule, then by a regime of self-discipline and fatherly love.

IV White redemption, Black mystery

In the end, Williams achieved manhood and mastery. But not quite. He did achieve broad popular acclaim, but he was still in a prison cell, and then he was executed. The world had the last word, and, from a theological perspective, Williams's story ends equivocally. Did he demonstrate world-transcending love? Or did he erect himself again as a god, making his own religion, composed of beliefs and practices that pleased him? (Among his spiritual practices, he prays facing toward Africa seven times a day 'or more, depending upon the spirit that moves me', 293.) How do we tell if redemption is motivated by desires for manliness, desires to make up for a compromised member, turning redemption narratives into a tool of masculinity rather than a means of overcoming masculinity?

Or, put provocatively: Does Williams's aspiration to be a good man really mask an aspiration to be a white man? His narrative might be read as advocating that excessively virile Black manliness, led by emotion and ultimately self-destructive, be traded in for a masculinity that is self-possessed, untroubled by excessive emotion, but also unexcited by the surprises and delights of the world. Traded in for a masculinity that loves self and family and friends, that believes in oneself, but that has too much faith and not enough hope. 'You can bend the most oppressive system to your will' (vii), Williams urges, but what of that which is uncertain, and of those powers that are mysterious? Could it not be that the rage Williams is so eager to keep in check is divine, pointing to the world's limits and the simultaneous necessity and impossibility of glimpsing beyond?

If there is a moral here, it is to avoid the genre of moralizing, and to be suspicious of the psychic dynamics that make moralizing attractive. It is tempting to lay out a path to redemption, at the social level through the termination of masculinity or white supremacy, or at the individual level through suppressing irrationality or rage or selfishness. Patriarchy, white supremacy, and other systems of domination are so grave that prediction and prescription necessarily entangle us in these same systems. Critical analysis of interlocking systems of domination is, indeed, necessary, but it must know its limits, and it must know where to direct its hopes. Those hopes must not be directed inward, at ourselves, but outward, at the struggles of communities most affected by domination. Their angry words and actions against domination form sacred texts, but like all such texts they are deeply opaque, deeply mysterious. The more we attempt to bring clarity rather than respond to mystery, the more genuine hope is lost.

Notes

1. Hortense Spillers, 'Papa's Baby, Mama's Maybe: An American Grammar Book', *Diacritics*, 17.2 (1987), 64–81.
2. Parenthetical numbering refers to pages in Stanley Tookie Williams, *Blue Rage, Black Redemption: A Memoir*, Pleasant Hill: Damamli Publishing Company, 2004.
3, There were some exceptions: Williams reports strong 'street' norms against rape (164), robbing churches (199), and collabourating with police (75).

Orthodox Ideology and Masculinity in Putin's Russia

In post-Soviet Russia, President Vladimir Putin has drawn from Orthodox ideology to promote and enact patriarchal constructions of masculinity. This article examines the hegemony of masculinity in the structures and practices of the Orthodox Church and argues that Putin's regime uses Orthodox teachings to defend its use of brutal force in domestic and foreign policies. The strategy of bellicose masculinity exposes the joint agenda of Church and state in Russia: to identify Russia as a safe space from the imaginary threat posed by the prospect of openness to Europe and the West.

I Introduction

In the post-Soviet period, Russia has turned to its past to refashion the historical foundation of its identity and its public image. Russian ideologues retrieved aspects of traditional Eastern Orthodox ideology to promote a neo-imperial agenda that would establish Russia as the most powerful state in Eurasia. Patriarchal constructions of masculinity are staple features of post-Soviet Russian identity, and the Russian Orthodox Church functioned as a convenient source for usable components of a powerful and patriarchal empire. Eastern Orthodoxy privileges the notion of an ideal family grounded by traditional values. In this paradigm, a strong male presides over families at the micro and macro-levels.

Russian president Vladimir Putin uses Orthodox teachings to promote masculinity in action and image. Putin executes masculinized policies of brutal force in the name of protecting and defending Russia from European secularism. Masculinity is central to Putin's neo-imperial strategy, as support for feminism and LGBTI rights are regarded as pillars of the European secularist agenda that threatens Russia's flourishing.

Putin's control over the Russian media results in the creation and dissemination of multiple poses depicting him as a throwback strongman.[1] Putin appears in photos as a participant in fierce athletic competitions, he is pictured in feral, natural settings, and displays his masculinity as a shirtless, bare-chested macho man.[2] Observers find humour in Putin's machismo, but the public display of masculinity is but one part of a larger, neo-imperial program celebrating the resurgence of Russia with strong men taking the lead in post-Soviet reconstruction.

This essay explores masculinity in aspects of Orthodox culture and ideology that contribute to Putin's program. It investigates expressions of masculinity in Orthodox structures and ritual practices, especially among the clergy. The essay also presents the limited admission of women to positions of power authorized by the Moscow Council of 1917–18, a movement forgotten in the post-Soviet era. The third part of this essay covers the feminist challenge posed to Orthodox masculinity in post-Soviet Russia by the punk band Pussy Riot, and the justification of violence in defending Russia from European secular values through the war in Ukraine.

II Masculinity in Orthodox structures, rituals, and ideology

The official structures of the Orthodox Church present expressions of masculinity, primarily through the holy orders, or ordained ministries. Only men can be candidates for ordination to these ministerial offices. Historically, women also exercised ministry in the major order of the deaconess. The deaconess's ministry differed from the deacons and was oriented towards women, and the order eventually fell into decline in the medieval period when infant baptism became predominant.[3]

The ritual differentiation of men and women is not limited to candidacy for ordination, however. The Byzantine Orthodox rite of baptism includes a rite of churching, typically concluding the process of baptism. The churching consists of the presbyter escorting the neophyte to the sanctuary. Boys and men are brought into the sanctuary area, circumambulating the altar while the presbyter recites the Canticle of Simeon. Girls and women are brought to the threshold of the sanctuary, without crossing it. The customary explanation for this gender differentiation is that the churching of men goes into the sanctuary to introduce males to the possibility that God may call them to presbyteral ministry. This explanation is theologically fatuous, as the rite of baptism and anointing is one of becoming a *laic*, a member of Christ's high priesthood, joining the assembly that exercises that priesthood in the altars of the Church and the world.[4] Despite the rare regional accommodation for churching girls in the sanctuary as well, the reservation of this practice for males only remains prevalent in Orthodoxy, punctuating the exclusivity of males as leaders in the structures of the Church.

From the perspective of the ordinary laic, then, all of the leadership functions of the Church are exercised by men. Ordained men preside at all services, proclaim the Gospel, preach, hear confessions, and impart Holy Communion. Orthodox culture also promotes reverence for the ordained clergy. Throughout the Church, it is traditional to ask a priest or bishop for a blessing, and to kiss his hand upon receiving it. Laics are expected to perform a prostration before a bishop before receiving his blessing and kissing his hand. Priests impart these blessings at the end of liturgical offices, holding the cross in the Slavic rite, and distributing *antidoron* (blessed bread) in the Greek rite at the end of the Divine Liturgy, with the laics kissing the hand.

One exception to this rule is in lay participation in the administration of the parish. In the Russian parish tradition, a lay leader known as a *starosta* (elder) assists the pastor in administering the community. The Moscow Council of 1917–18 permitted women to function as parish *starostas* as part of its platform for renewal and reinvigorating the laity's participation in Church life.[5] The Council also permitted women to serve as diocesan representatives and become psaltists.[6] This groundbreaking council, however, was interrupted and stifled by the fierce persecution of the Church by the Bolsheviks. The reformed principles of the Moscow Council did not take root in the Russian Church of the Soviet era, so patriarchal constructions of masculinity remained ensconced in the Church's structures and values. These patriarchal structures and values became prominent in Russia's post-Soviet identity.

III Post-soviet Russian Orthodoxy and neo-imperialism

Contemporary conservatism in Russian Orthodoxy is located in two compatible ideological platforms: the *Russkii Mir*, or Russian World initiative of current Patriarch Kirill, and the comprehensive document presenting a systematic definition of the Russian Church's theological ethics, the Basis of the Social Concept of the Russian Orthodox Church.[7] The Russian World ideology and the social document are key ideological pillars of Putin's vision for Russia's pre-eminence in Eurasia in the post-Soviet epoch.

The Russian World is relevant to our topic because of its reliance on the traditional values of Russia's past, including patriarchal constructions of masculinity. Patriarch Kirill defines the Russian World as a global Orthodox civilization grounded in the heritage and values of Russia's golden age, beginning with the medieval city-states of Rus' and continuing through the Russian Empire up until its collapse in 1917. Patriarch Kirill presents the Russian World as a traditional defence against the secular humanism unleashed by globalization. Orthodox Christians whose values are incompatible with secular humanism will find their true home in the Russian World, because the Russian World offers a safe haven from secular humanism's illusion of human progress.

The patriarch defines the Russian World as a multinational community with walls and borders. Russia, Belarus, and Ukraine are the founding nations of the Russian World, but it embraces anyone. One becomes a citizen of the Russian World through the Moscow Patriarchate. Russian is the official language of communication, and Church Slavonic is the language of prayer. The borders of the Russian World reconnect the countries that were part of the pre-revolutionary Russian Empire and were important republics of the Soviet Union. The borders of Patriarch Kirill's Russian World align conveniently with Russian pre-eminence in Eurasia, and Russian culture dominates, since Moscow is the capital, and Russian is the language of communication.

The Basis of the Social Concept of the Russian Orthodox Church is the official document presenting the teachings and core values of the Russian World. Masculinity is a pillar of the social concept because it promotes the model of a strong male overseeing households at the micro- and macro-levels. In the section on personal, family, and public

77

morality, the document canonizes gender complementarity and difference while upholding the equality of women to men. The document is careful to emphasize that equality does not exclude gender difference, and that the Church upholds the calling of women to be wives and mothers. This section asserts patriarchal constructions of masculinity by emphasizing the traditional role of the husband as the head of the wife, and the wife's responsibility to obey her husband from the Ephesians pericope appointed to the office of crowning (marriage) in the Orthodox rite. According to the document, women are equal, but also subordinate to men. Their calling is to be wives and mothers, and noble, dignified, and distinct, as only men are divinely appointed to lead in domestic and ecclesial communities, an image of classic patriarchy manifest in the Orthodox Church's liturgical tradition.

The social concept document's rejection of homosexuality as a sexual orientation is another instance of privileging masculinity in households. The document argues that homosexuality is a vicious distortion of the God-created human nature that can be overcome by spiritual effort.[8] This section is important because it refers to the foundational pillar of humanity as man and woman, with this gender complementarity divinely appointed: 'The Orthodox Church proceeds from the invariable conviction that the divinely established marital union of man and woman cannot be compared to the perverted manifestations of sexuality.' The Russian Church likewise condemns transsexuality and permits baptism of transsexuals only in their original sex, while prohibiting ordination of transsexuals. Any deviation from the divinely appointed patriarchal paradigm is prohibited, evinced by the Church's belief that 'those who propagate the homosexual way of life should not be admitted to educational and other work with children and youth, nor to occupy superior posts in the army and reformatories.'[9] The document is designed to legitimize and privilege masculinity at the micro- and macro-levels, especially when prototypical masculine actions are employed to defend Russia from the European threat.

The social concept document does not openly call for the subjugation of women to men. In its retrieval of Russian traditional values, the document promotes male-female gender complementarity that includes some mutually exclusive roles as divinely appointed and therefore unchangeable. This ideological principle fits in with the Russian World as a multinational society that promotes moral rigour against the threats posed by the secular humanism promoted by the West. The hegemony of the moral ideal and its implications for gender relations is therefore a primary identity marker of Russia as an empire preserving traditional moral values. The post-Soviet preference for patriarchal constructions of masculinity legitimized the state's crackdown on feminist challenges and the use of military force to destabilize Ukraine. In both instances, masculinization was employed, with an assist from the Orthodox Church, to pit a strong Russia against its weak, feminine opponents who sought to pollute Russia with feminism and its depravity.

IV Threats to the Russian World and masculine responses

There have been two formidable challenges to the neo-imperial dominance of the Russian World and its overt masculinity, one within Russia, and one outside of it. The punk band Pussy Riot presented the first direct challenge through their public prayer service performance in Christ the Saviour Cathedral in 2012.[10] The Ukrainian people presented the second challenge, primarily through the Maidan revolution, and secondarily through the attainment of canonical autocephaly from the patriarch of Constantinople in 2018–19. Russia responded in both cases through hybrid war, waging a brutal assault on the perpetrators physically and through the media.

Pussy Riot's performance caricatured Patriarch Kirill and the Church as Putin's puppets in their happy marginalization of all misfits and outcasts, especially women and the LGBT community. The band stood on the solea of Christ the Saviour Cathedral, beginning their punk performance with a melodic motif from Rachmaninov's setting of 'Rejoice, o Virgin, mother of God', no. 6 from his famous *Vespers*. Pussy Riot altered the lyrics, singing 'O Mother of God, Virgin, banish Putin!' The rest of the song mocks Patriarch Kirill for blind sycophantism, hoarding wealth, stealing the people's freedom, and disregarding and discarding the marginalized of Russian society.[11]

The timing of this performance is crucial: it occurred just a few months after the historic visit of the belt worn by Mary, the Mother of God, to Moscow. Muscovites had waited in line for days in the cold to have a chance to venerate the belt in the cathedral, and the Church used the opportunity to invite the people into the Church, distributing copies

79

of Mary's belt and disseminating stories of miraculous healings and conceptions that had occurred within the short time-frame of the visit. Pussy Riot's invocation of Mary throughout the punk performance called upon Mary not to perform miracles, but to banish Putin and become a feminist, placing Mary, Mother of God, among the marginalized dismissed by Putin and the Church because they represent a threat to the moral fibre of the Russian World.[12]

In Orthodox liturgy and piety, Mary bears many titles, including *Strategios*, the general of an army that defends God's people. To this day, Orthodox people call upon Mary to defeat their enemies, carrying her icon into battle and attributing victories to her protection. Pussy Riot's appeal for Mary to banish Putin and become a feminist is an act of subversion that exposes the masculine features of Putin's regime and the Russian Church. The song pleads with Mary to remove the patriarch and president who expel the marginalized, depicting Mary as an advocate for the marginalized, and not for those who adhere to traditional patriarchal values.[13]

The Russian government acted swiftly in condemning Pussy Riot's performance as a criminal act of hooliganism, sentencing them to two years in prison. Representatives of the Church harshly condemned their performance as blasphemous and offensive, an opinion held by ordinary Russian citizens as well. The Pussy Riot incident was one of the few incidents of a grassroots challenge to the establishment of the Russian World – Putin and Patriarch Kirill – that came from within Russia. A similar situation unfolded at the Olympics in Sochi in 2014 when the punk band seized the opportunity for another prophetic challenge. In this instance, the official response was in an instance of brutal masculinity, as a special ensemble of Cossack police pursued the band members, with one male officer publicly whipping band members during the dispersal.[13]

Pussy Riot's performances were subversive acts that called out the alliance of Church and state, especially since three band members performed a forbidden punk prayer service at a location in the cathedral that prohibited women for public performance. The use of brutal force to end the Sochi performance and publicly humiliate the band symbolizes the masculine character of Putin's Russia, especially with the male officer beating female performers.[14] Supporters of the crackdown on Pussy Riot justified their actions on the basis of the accusation that Pussy Riot's feminist agenda would introduce the depravity of Western secularism to Russia.[15] The masculine ideology of post-Soviet Russia condemns the feminism of Pussy Riot while honouring 'Putin's Army', a group of young women who express their support for Putin through erotic imagery.[16] The women posing for Putin project an image of the proper space and role of women in the Russian World. Women are to satisfy the needs of men in the world dominated by masculinity; challenges to the masculine-dominant paradigm are prohibited and will be attacked with brutal force.[17]

This scene unfolded on a larger scale with broader geopolitical implications during the Ukrainian Euromaidan Revolution in 2013–14. While the diverse group of people that assembled on independence square were protesting the Ukrainian president, the movement was a veritable rejection of the Russian World.[18] Participants in the Maidan Revolution sought to build a new Ukraine on the basis of dignity, non-violence, transparency, and accountability.[19] They envisioned Ukraine as a core country of the European Union, an aspiration that posed a threat to Putin's neo-imperial agenda. Historically, Central and Western European literature, music, and values entered Russia via Ukraine as the country bordering both Poland and Russia, a legacy of cultural influence with which Russian ideologues were intimately familiar. Putin and Patriarch Kirill's Russian World identified Ukraine as a crucial cell of the Orthodox civilization, and the Ukrainian people's determination to join Europe instead of Putin's Eurasian project was construed by Russia as an act of betrayal. The photos and videos capture the drama of the confrontation between the people and the Berkut riot police. The death of one hundred innocents resulted in the valourization of the heavenly hundred.

But the Maidan was only the beginning of bloodshed. Russia responded to Ukraine's decision to embrace the West as an evil act of betrayal. Putin annexed Crimea by force and waged a war in Donbas that has resulted in over 13,000 casualties and the displacement of 1.5 million people – an enduring human catastrophe.

While Putin publicly denies Russia's role in the war, it is supported by mainstream Russian clergy. Mikhail Suslov's research on the sentiments of clergy and laity on the Ukrainian revolution and ensuing war in Donbas disclose the justification for bellicose action.[20] Ukraine's choice for the West violated the core values holding the Russian World together. A vote for Europe was a vote for secular humanism and all of the threats to Orthodoxy that accompany it, especially feminism and the pro-gay lobby. Depicting the Maidan as an event where Ukrainians betrayed not only Russians, their brothers in the faith, but also the Orthodox faith they hold in common, was possible only if the devil had taken possession of the Ukrainian people.[21] The only solution was to remove the evil threat from the Russian World, with the understanding that Ukraine belongs to Russia in the post-Soviet ideological scheme.

Cyril Hovorun demonstrates how the Russian Orthodox Church supported Putin in transforming the Russian World ideology into a political religion that turned to terrorism in its campaign of Occidentalism.[22] The use of brutal military force would excise the evil threat posed by European secularism in Ukraine from the sanctity of the Russian World. The anti-Ukrainian enmity was also cause for official representatives of the Russian Church to bless soldiers who would fight in Russia's war against the devil in Ukraine, resulting in the creation of a 'Russian Orthodox army'.[23] Raising an army of men to defend the values of the Russian World threatened by Ukraine's flirtation with Europe was the only action befitting the masculine strongman leading Russia who held on to his position of power by force, and imposed his power not only in Russia and Ukraine, but also in Georgia. The fight was not merely a matter of saving Ukraine from Europe. The sanctity of the micro- and macro-level masculine strongholds that function as apparatuses of the Russian World were at stake. The men who forced Ukraine to remain subordinate to the Russian World were attempting to protect the ideal male household paradigm from the corruption of feminist and LGBTI threats. By appealing to the right to defend its people and protect its national interests in the Ukrainian crisis, both Russia's Occidentalism and systematic masculinization were exposed.[24]

V Conclusion

Putin's Russia depends on the reconstitution of select components of the past. Today's Russia draws upon an assemblage of ideas from the past that envision Russia as the guardian of traditional moral rigour, defended by Church representatives as a safe haven for those who feel threatened by the secular humanism preponderant in the West. The promotion of gender differentiation and complementarity, in which the male rules over submissive females has ascended to the heights of Russia's ideological platform. This ideology celebrates Putin as a contemporary icon of masculinity, a strong man who seeks power, exercises it with cold calculation and brutality, and justifies the use of power by appealing to the masculine responsibilities of protecting rights and defending people.

Patriarch Kirill's cultivation of the Russian World ideology that emphasizes traditional moral rigour proved to be a convenient and compatible foundation for Putin's reign. The Russian World would restore Muscovite dominance over Eurasia, one Moscow had held during the Soviet era, while justifying brutal measures employed to protect adherents of the Russian World from demonic threats from the West. The tactics used to eradicate these threats symbolize the classic form of bellicose masculinity: men apprehending women, publicly beating them, and organizing armies to crush their enemies outside of their borders, despite the wailing of Russian mothers whose sons died in the campaign. It seems ironic that the ruling regime of post-Soviet Russia would turn to such brutal measures against its neighbours in the wake of seventy years of violent Soviet persecution of the people. It is tragic that these measures find support in the resurgence of traditional patriarchy in Russia's Orthodox Church.

Notes

1. See Valerie Sperling, 'Putin's Macho Personality Cult', *Communist and Post-communist Studies*, 49 (2016), 14–15.
2. See Andrew Foxall, 'Photographing Vladimir Putin: Masculinity, Nationalism and Visuality in Russian Political Culture', *Geopolitics*, 18 (2018), 132–156, doi: 10.1080/14650045.2012.713245.
3. Readers should note that the male diaconate also declined during this period.
4. On this matter, see Carrie Frederick Frost, *Maternal Body: A Theology of Incarnation from the Christian East*, foreword by Julie Hanlon Rubio, Mahwah: Paulist Press, 2019, pp. 52–65.
5. Hyacinthe Destivelle, *The Moscow Council (1917–1918): The Creation of the Conciliar Institutions of the Russian Orthodox Church*, edited by Michael Plekon and Vitaly Permiakov, translated by Jerry Ryan, South Bend: University of Notre Dame, 2015, p. 105.
6. Destivelle, *The Moscow Council*, p. 327. A psaltist leads the singing and reads from the psalter and the Epistle in many parishes. The council stipulated that women could be psaltsists in 'special cases', and were not permitted to become members of the clergy.
7. On the Russian World, see Cyril Hovorun, 'Interpreting the Russian World', in Andrii

Krawchuk and Thomas Bremer (eds.), *Churches in the Ukrainian Crisis*, Cham: Palgrave Macmillan, 2016, pp. 163–172. See also Nicholas Denysenko, 'Fractured Orthodoxy in Ukraine and Politics: The Impact of Patriarch Kyrill's "Russian World"', *Logos: A Journal of Eastern Christian Studies*, 54.1–2 (2013), 33–68. The social concept document can be accessed here: https://mospat.ru/en/documents/social-concepts/.

8. 'Homosexual desires, just as other passions torturing fallen man, are healed by the Sacraments, prayer, fasting, repentance, reading of Holy Scriptures and patristic writings, as well as Christian fellowship with believers who are ready to give spiritual support' (https://mospat.ru/en/documents/social-concepts/).

9. https://mospat.ru/en/documents/social-concepts/.

10. See Janet Elise Johnson, 'Pussy Riot as a Feminist Project: Russia's Gendered Informal Politics', *Nationalist Papers*, 42 (2014), 583-90; Vera Shevzov, 'Women on the Fault Lines of Faith: Pussy Riot and the insider/outsider Challenge to Russian Orthodoxy', Religion and Gender, 4 (2014), 121–44; and Nicholas Denysenko, 'An Appeal to Mary: An Analysis of Pussy Riot's Punk Performance in Moscow', *Journal of the American Academy of Religion*, 81.4 (2013), 1061–1092.

11. See a good translation by Jeffrey Tayler, 'What Pussy Riots "Punk Prayer" Really Said', https://www.theatlantic.com/international/archive/2012/11/what-pussy-riots-punk-prayer-really-said/264562/.

12. On the Russian Church's aversion to feminism, see Shevzov, 'Women on the Fault Lines', 125–126.

13. Andrew Roth, 'Cossacks with Horse Whips Attack Members of Russian Protest Group', *New York Times*, 20 February 2014 (A4).

14. For a discussion of the Russian church's role in opposing feminism, see Johnson, 'Pussy Riot as a Feminist Project', 585. For an explanation of the Russian people's hesitance to endorse the punk prayer performance, see Shevzov, 'Women on the Fault Lines', 132–135.

15. See Oleg Riabov and Tatiana Riabova, 'The Remasculinization of Russia? Gender, Nationalism, and the Legitimation of Power under Vladimir Putin', *Problems of Post-communism*, 61 (2014), 31–32.

16. Foxall, 'Photographing Vladimir Putin'.

17. For expert analysis on the contributions of women within the post-Soviet Russian Orthodox Church in spite of their narrowly defined spaces, see Nadieszda Kizenko, 'Feminized Patriarchy? Orthodoxy and Gender in Post-Soviet Russia', *Signs*, 38.3 (2013), 595–621.

18. Catherine Wanner, 'Orthodoxy and the Future of Secularism after the Maidan', *Euxeinos*, 17 (2015), 9.

19. Anatoly Akhutin and Irina Berlyand, 'Maidan as Event', *Russian Studies in Philosophy*, 54 (2016), 244–246.

20. Mikhail Suslov, 'The Russian Orthodox Church and the Crisis in Ukraine', in Andrii Krawchuk and Thomas Bremer (eds.), *Churches in the Ukrainian Crisis*, Cham: Palgrave Macmillan, 2016, pp. 133–162.

21. Suslov, 'The Crisis in Ukraine', pp. 150–152.

22. See Cyril Hovorun, *Political Orthodoxies: The Unorthodoxies of the Church Coerced*, Minneapolis: Fortress Press, 2018.

23. Hovorun treats the role of the Church in supporting Putin's antics in *Political Orthodoxies*, pp. 72–87. He exposes the Church's public support for violence and bloodshed on pp. 94–99.

24. See Sperling, 'Putin's Macho Personality Cult', 16–17.

Transcending Gender:
Colonialism, Gandhi and Religion

SHYAM PAKHARE

Gandhi was a deeply religious person. His political, social and economic thoughts sprang from spirituality, in the backdrop of colonialism. Gandhi had experienced the transformative influence of religion on people and understood the ability of religion 'to make men out of straw'. In the colonial context, Hindu men were derided as 'mild' by the British, establishing a hegemony of imperialist British masculinity. Gandhi made Indians feel proud about the gentleness of their nature. He aspired to transcend gender binaries. Gandhi appealed to the conscience of the Colonial masters through satyagraha. *It was not a war but a conversation. There was no victor and no vanquished. It was a collective journey towards truth.*

I Introduction

The age of enlightenment, characterized by scientism, rationalism and materialism, created a binary between religion and material world. Darwin's theory of evolution and the philosophy of utilitarianism developed a rift in the organic lifestyle of the west. 'Knowledge is power' and 'survival of the fittest' were the new mantras of this age. It separated human life from nature leading to an ideology of anthropocentrism based on the superiority of human beings over other species and dominance over the nature. It had its cascading effect on human society also. Respect towards nature and many other noble sentiments of human beings were the victims of the modern age. Colonialism was an outcome of the process which led to further binaries – colonizers and colonized. Gender played an important role in the process of colonization. It had been long neglected in the research on modern India. This article is an attempt to study Gandhi's thoughts on religion from the perspective of gender and explore its impact in the struggle for independence.

II Muscular Christianity

According to Raewyn Connell, there is a dimension of masculinity in the culture of imperialism, and empires have been a gendered enterprise from the start.[1] The British invasion of India was not merely a material invasion but an invasion of a very different civilization. It was a clash between two very different visions of life. All the organized religions were founded and dominated by men, but the core of every religion remained feminine, emphasizing values such as love, harmony and compassion. Masculinity is not static – it is constantly reconstructed. The aggressive model of masculinity became dominant after the mid-nineteenth century. In the modern age, the colonial powers tried to wipe out the feminine values from Christianity because they were incompatible with the exploitative nature of colonialism. Masculine values were given superior status over feminine values. The colonizers were considered as masculine and the colonized as feminine. The expansion of the British Empire was defended as a civilizing mission and soldiers and adventurers were celebrated as heroes. Rudyard Kipling glorified colonialism as 'White man's burden'.

Muscular Christianity was an outcome of this process. It first developed in England and the United States and was intimately linked to colonialism.[2] Muscular Christianity provided a moral justification for the exploitation of the people in Asia and Africa. It considered cultivating physical strength through sports and exercise as a means to character building. Earlier religion had been a matter of inner conscience, but in the age of colonialism it was expected to serve the interests of the material world. It left an impact on the religious perceptions of the colonized people living in urban areas where socio-religious reform movements originated and had to grapple with the muscular orientation of religion newly introduced by the colonial masters.

III Psychological invasion and a dilemma

Colonialism was more a psychological invasion than a physical one. A few thousand British could not rule millions of Indians for about 200 years with mere physical prowess. An inferiority complex had to be inculcated in the minds of the colonized to subjugate their minds. Colonialism was an interplay of masculinities. A propaganda was launched to impress on Indians that they were weak, effeminate and unfit to rule themselves. One influential leader of the Indian National Congress, Lala Lajpat Rai (1865–1928) rightly observed that political, physical and economic emasculation was the key to British rule in India.[3] Imperialist historians like James Mill and Vincent A. Smith, and journalists like Katherine Mayo acted as agents of this propaganda. Indians took pride in their religions. But James Mill (1773–¬1836), author of *The History of British India*, unjustly criticized Hindu religion. He called Indians 'rude' and 'uncivilized'. He also ridiculed the gentleness of manners of Indians. He wrote, 'In truth, the Hindu, *like the Eunuch*, excels in the qualities of a slave.'[4]

Allen Greenberger in his famous book *The British Image of India* points out that the image of effeminate Indians, especially effeminate Hindu, and masculine British was created in the fictional works of that time. It had its effect not only in England but also in India. The British went to India with this prejudice, which was one of the major reasons for the lack of understanding between the British and Indians.[5] This led to the development of British hegemonic masculinity and subordinated Indian masculinity.

The hegemony of the model of muscular Christianity was established. It posed a serious challenge in front of the elites in Hindu society who resided in towns and cities and had been defining Hinduism for generations. But Indians living in villages and the socio-religious life of rural area did not face the direct onslaught of muscular Christianity. The elite class of Indians living in towns and cities responded to the challenge through revivalist and reformist approaches. The revivalist religious reform movements, such as Arya Samaj, incorporated many traits of Christian missionaries and aggressively criticized Christianity along with other religions and even different cults within Hinduism. It appeared more like a missionary version of Hinduism. Swami Vivekananda also tried to transform Hinduism into muscular Hinduism on the model of muscular

Christianity. He held physical weakness responsible for the miseries of India and asked Indian men to build 'muscles of iron and nerves of steel' and then turn to religion. He even advised men to follow a non-vegetarian diet to build physical strength. The Western impact was quite visible in the outlook of reformist socio-religious movements also. These movements originated in urban areas and did not have much influence on rural areas. Revivalists or reformists could not capture the imagination of the rural population because none of them had evolved from indigenous traditions and appeared to them as alien as Christianity. Gandhi's religious ideas developed in this context.

IV Gandhi's religion: A global experience

Gandhi was born and brought up in a Vaishnav family of the princely state of Porbandar in the Kathiawad region of India, away from the direct intervention of the colonial power and the socio-religious reform movements of British India. There was a liberal religious atmosphere in his family. There were followers of Jainism in Porbandar, and the principles of Jainism, like non-violence, chastity, non-stealing and non-possession, left a deep impact on Gandhi in his formative years. The evolution of Gandhi's religious thoughts was the outcome of a global experience. His stays in London and South Africa, and his lifelong interaction with the followers of different religions made him accepting of social differences. He assimilated noble thoughts of all religions in his idea of Hinduism. There was a meeting of East and West in his religious thought. He said that the revelation of passive resistance came to him after reading the Sermon on the Mount in 1893. In 1920, when an English clergyman asked Gandhi about the book which influenced him most, he replied that it was the New Testament. Tolstoy played a major role in shaping Gandhi's religious outlook. In his book *The Kingdom of God Is within You*,[6] Tolstoy criticized the institutional Christian church and its role in spreading idolatrous rituals and blind beliefs among the people. Tolstoy emphasized good works instead of ritualized sacraments and prayer. He also criticized muscular Christianity and its attempt to reconcile Christian teaching with the use of force.

Gandhi was a deeply religious person whose religiosity affected all facets of his life. However, his political, social and economic thoughts sprang from his religious ideas on the backdrop of colonialism. For him, the struggle against racial discrimination in South Africa and against colonialism in India was a spiritual endeavour. Gandhi considered belief in God as one of the indispensable qualifications to be a *satyagrahi*, or seeker of truth. He was liberal enough to accommodate different perceptions of religion in his religious worldview. He even considered the belief of an atheist in atheism as religion.[7]

Gandhi believed that all religions were more or less true. All proceeded from the same God and all were imperfect. He disapproved the efforts of some Christian missionaries to win over converts to Christianity. He considered it a kind of invasion. Gandhi firmly believed that no one should convert to another religion but try their best to reform one's own religion. He also said that if a Hindu wanted to believe in the Bible, they should do it but there was no reason for disregarding their own religion. In other words, Gandhi was a pluralist who believed that one could hold multiple religious traditions to be true.[7]

V Masculine reason versus feminine faith

Gandhi gave due weight to reason but also believed that where reason could not take one far, things had to be accepted on faith. Faith did not contradict reason but could transcend it. He believed that God did not merely satisfy the intellect but ruled the heart and transformed it. Rationalism had been the foundation of enlightenment leading to modern age and was considered by that age to be an attribute of masculinity. Moderates, Extremists and Revolutionary Nationalists in India also had accepted the superiority of reason. It created mental barrier around their thinking by deepening the binary between reason and faith. Such a rationalist anti-colonial approach was not successful in their struggle against colonialism. Gandhi rejected the supremacy of reason and gave hope to the people in the form of faith in the justice of the cause and God. Faith which is based on emotions has a feminine connotation. He said that faith in oneself was synonymous with faith in God. If the people of India had faith, they would cease to fear one another. Fear of the colonial power and the sense of helplessness in front of it were the main reasons behind the British dominance over India. It created the mental image of British as overpowering and masculine and of Indian men as helpless and effeminate. Mrinalini Sinha has called both notions of masculinities together colonial masculinities.[8]

Gandhi had realized the power of religion during his struggle in South Africa. In 1906, in a public meeting called to protest against a humiliating ordinance, one speaker named Haji Habib said that Indians must pass the resolution against the ordinance with God as witness and must never yield in cowardly submission to such degrading legislation. It created a sensation among the Hindus and Muslims present in that meeting. In his speech during the meeting, Gandhi said, 'To pledge ourselves or to take an oath in the name of God or with Him as witness is not something to be trifled with. If having taken such oath, we violate our pledge, we are guilty before God and man. Personally, I hold that a man, who deliberately and intelligently takes a pledge and then breaks it, forfeits his manhood'.[9] At the end of the meeting all present, standing with upraised hands, took an oath with God as witness not to submit to the Ordinance. After many years Gandhi wrote about this incident, 'I can never forget the scene, which is present before my mind's eyes as I write.'[10] Later in life, as a supreme leader of Indian Freedom Struggle, Gandhi always projected the mass movement against the British colonialism as a religious duty of Indians. He understood the pulse of masses and knew the transformative effect of religion on Indians and the ability of religion to make 'men out of straw'.

Faith in God rescued Gandhi from the dilemma of whether to follow British law or not. He considered the voice of conscience (inner voice) the most important criterion to take a decision or chart out any course of action. He called this inner voice divinely inspired, it stood above the law of the land. It liberated him mentally and physically. In 1917, when he was presented in front of magistrate for the trial for disobeying the order to leave Champaran, he said, 'I have disregarded the order served upon me not for want of respect for lawful authority, but in obedience to the higher law of our being, the voice of conscience.'[11] In 1930, he projected his march to Dandi to break the unjust salt act as a sacred pilgrimage. In 1942, before the passage of the Quit India Resolution, he asked members of the Congress Working Committee to take a pledge with God and one's conscience as witness. He said that through the movement, people would appeal to the highest tribunal of justice. Human law, thus, was always in service of divine law.

VI Spiritualization of politics

Gandhi believed that the modern age was the age of politics because almost all the aspects of individual and social life were directly or indirectly organized and administered by the state. As a result, he thought that there was need for the spiritualization of political life and political institutions as a means to serve humanity. With this conviction he entered the political field. But he rejected the attempt of politicizing religion by leaders like Lokmanya Tilak (1856–1920, supreme political leader of India before Gandhi's rise) who had introduced the public celebration of Ganesh festival as a means to generate unrest against the British rule. Gandhi led an aggressive ideological battle against Tilak who did not consider Gandhi as a politician and called him a *sadhu* (saint). Tilak said that politics was not a game of *sadhus* but of worldly people. Gandhi retorted, 'The epitome of all religions is to promote *purushartha* and *purushartha* is nothing but a desperate attempt to become a *sadhu*, i.e., to become a gentleman in every sense of the term'.[12] Unlike Tilak, Gandhi wanted women also to do *purushartha*. It was impossible without the fearlessness which Gandhi called the first requisite for spiritual conduct. Gandhi criticized Tilak's policy that 'everything is fair in politics' and the maxim of 'evil in return for evil'. Instead he said that there should be good in return for evil. He believed in the inviolable connection between the means and the end and the maxim that one reaps what one sows. As he considered India's struggle for freedom a spiritual endeavour, he was emphatic about the purity of means.

He also rejected Tilak's interpretation of the *Bhagvad Gita*. Tilak had written a critique of the *Gita* titled *Gitarahasya*[13] in which he argued that the *Gita* taught selfless action, *karmayoga*. Gandhi did not agree with Tilak and said instead that the *Gita* taught non-violence and renunciation, *anasaktiyoga*. He was trying to de-emphasize masculine Hinduism and create a different space for an inclusive one. It was indeed a difficult task because in Hindu mythology and in visual representation, Hindu Gods and Goddesses have been shown armed with different weapons. Hindu epics and mythologies are replete with battles between rulers and between Gods and demons. Gandhi understood that indirectly Tilak and other leaders of Congress were trying to imitate models of muscular masculinity practiced by the colonial masters. He pointed out that in the process they were

91

sacrificing their unique identity as Indians.

Gandhi also had to fight many ideological battles against right wing *Hindutva* ideologues (those who believed in Hindu majoritarianism) and Muslim leaders who used religion to serve their separatist communal agenda. He believed in the doctrine of *Advaita* (non-dualism), which means unity of existence. He understood the binaries present in the modern age, such as man and nature, masculine and feminine, living and non-living things, East and West, and strove to go beyond them in search of common ground. Based in his belief in non-dualism, he would not let the British do injustice because they were an integral and inseparable part of humanity, and would not let Indians unleash hate on the British that would compromise their humanity. *Moksha* (liberation) was the ultimate aim which had to be attained through being part of society and with mutual help. Hence, he gave importance to community living and collective prayer. Gandhi did not want religion reduced to a Saturday or Sunday affair. He wanted people to live it in every moment. Gandhi had faith that human nature in its essence was one and, therefore, unfailingly responded to the advances of love. For him, even Hitler and Mussolini were not beyond redemption. It could be possible only with self-suffering and not by hatred.

According to Gandhi, one could cultivate renunciation by observing the vows of truth, non-violence, celibacy, non-stealing, non-possession and control of the senses. For him, independence of India was just a milestone in the long journey towards *swaraj* or *Ramraj* (Kingdom of God), which he defined as rule over self and its base desires. By inculcating these values, one could gain the soul force which was the only weapon at hand for Indians in this unequal battle against the mighty British empire. Gandhi never expected India to practice non-violence out of weakness. It had to be practiced being conscious of one's strength and power. He believed that soul force made human beings fearless even when facing guns and cannons. Gandhi witnessed two world wars and destruction caused by atomic weapons. He believed that modern science and technology bereft of human values had led to armed cowardice because in modern warfare humans never came face to face with the enemies. Soul force was an inclusive and accessible power which could be practiced by all: women, the aged and children. Soul force does not capitulate to subjugation.

Gandhi called it a new *kshatriya* (warrior) spirit. It made the practitioner fearless and struck at the roots of colonialism.

Violence was visible in many prevalent socio-religious practices of Hinduism. It was present in social relationships between men and women, between upper caste and lower caste relations, between the rich and the poor in India. Gandhi advocated that Hinduism had to be purged of its inhuman practices to gain soul force. Injustices heaped on women, dalits and indigenous peoples had to be done away with. Gandhi gave women equal status in society and invited them to participate in the struggle for independence as equal partners. He redefined the concept of masculinity and asked men to incorporate the best feminine qualities. He did not believe that imbibing positive feminine qualities made man effeminate. He also expected women to inculcate positive masculine qualities such as confidence and courage.

For Gandhi, God was not a person, but an eternal principle. For him, God was truth and truth was God. He said that even the atheist did not doubt the necessity of truth and that in their own way, they were in search of the divine. *Satyagraha* therefore was a search for truth, for God. Gandhi called it a *Dharmayuddha* (righteous warfare). In this form of spiritual warfare, non-cooperation and civil disobedience were like branches of the tree called *satyagraha*. On this path, the only way to truth was to be non-violent, even to one's oppressor. *Satyagraha* was an attribute of the spirit within, which was latent in everyone. As one person could not claim understanding of the whole truth, *satyagraha* gave some credit for honesty of purpose to the opponents also. *Satyagraha* became a medium of conversation. One who followed *satyagraha* wanted to convert the opponent to their view and at the same time was ready to be converted if they thought that the opponent had convincing argument based on truth. In *satyagraha*, no one was victor and no one was vanquished. It was a communal journey towards truth. Independence was the realization of the 'Kingdom of God within oneself' for both the colonizers and the colonized. It would help the colonial masters to liberate themselves from the dichotomy of noble Christian values and the un-Christian acts of exploiting the colonies. *Satyagraha* refined masculinity and femininity as a spiritual search for truth.

VII Conclusion

Hindu men were derided as 'mild' by the British. Gandhi's model of masculinity made Indians feel proud about their cultural ethos. Gandhi made Indians feel proud about the gentleness of their nature. He also made them realize that gentleness was not a sign of weakness but a sign of strength, the legacy of their age-old civilization. Indians across the social spectrum responded positively to Gandhi's reframing of masculinity and femininity, and of oppressor and oppressed. The non-dualism that Gandhi advocated existed in Hindu practices of non-binary forms of deities. Worshipping *Ardhanarishwar* (the composite male-female figure of the Hindu God Shiva with his consort Parvati representing fusion of *purusha* [masculine] and *prakriti* [feminine]) has been prevalent in India since ancient times. *Shakti* (power) has always been considered as feminine quality in India.

Gandhi faced aggressive colonial masculinity by combining positive masculine and feminine qualities which can be called androgynous. It would make a person a complete human being transcending gender binaries. He tried to restore the feminine core of religion with values such as love, compassion and harmony.

Gandhi's influence originated from his spirituality. For the masses he was foremost a *Mahatma* (a great soul). It had its unmatched impact on the people. Gilbert Murray rightly remarked on Gandhi in 1914: 'Persons in power should be very careful how they deal with a man who cares nothing for sensual pleasure, nothing for riches, nothing for comfort or praise or promotion, but is simply determined to do what he believes to be right. He is a dangerous and uncomfortable enemy, because his body which you can always conquer, gives you so little purchase upon his soul.'[14] Gandhi left a message behind for the oppressed and downtrodden of the world to look inward and realize this soul force to gain strength against injustice.

Notes

1. Raewyn W. Connell, *Masculinities*, Berkeley: University of California Press, 2005, p. xvi.
2. Joseph S. Alter, 'Indian Clubs and Colonialism: Hindu Masculinity and Muscular Christianity', *Comparative Studies in Society and History*, 46.3 (2004), 497–534.
3. Lajpat Rai, Young India, 4th reprint, *Lahore: Servants of the People Society*, 1927, p. 46.
4. James Mill, *History of British India*, vol. 2, London: Baldwin, Cradock & Joy, 1826, p. 457 (emphasis added).
5. Allen Greenberger, *The British Image of India: A Study in the Literature of Imperialism 1880-1960*, London: Oxford University Press, 1969, pp. 11–12.
6. Leo Tolstoy, *The Kingdom of God Is within You*, translated by Constance Garnett, New York: Cassell Publishing, 1894. The book left a deep impact on Gandhi's spiritual thoughts.
7. Dinanath Gopal Tendulkar, *Mahatma: Life of Mohandas Karamchand Gandhi*, vol. 4, Bombay: Vithalbhai K. Jhaveri & D. G. Tendulkar, 1952, pp. 121–127, 166–173.
8. Mrinalini Sinha, *Colonial Masculinity: The 'Manly Englishman' and the 'Effeminate Bengali' in the Late Nineteenth Century*, Manchester and New York: Manchester University Press, 1995, p. 2.
9. Mohandas Karamchand Gandhi, *The Selected Works of Mahatma Gandhi*, vol. 2, translated by Valji Govindji Desai, Ahmedabad: Navjivan Publishing House, 1968, p. 114.
10. Gandhi, *The Selected Works*, p. 117.
11. Dinanath Gopal Tendulkar, *Mahatma: Life of Mohandas Karamchand Gandhi*, vol. 1, Bombay: Vithalbhai K. Jhaveri & D. G. Tendulkar, 1951, p. 250.
12. *The Collected Works of Mahatma Gandhi*, vol.16, Ahmedabad: The Publications Division, Ministry of Information and Broadcasting, Government of India, 1965, pp. 490–491. *Purushartha* is an important aspect of Hinduism. It expects a human being to follow four aims in his life – *dharma* (moral duty), *artha* (economic prosperity), *kaam* (pleasure) and *moksha* (liberation from the cycle of life and birth). But it was not a universal ideal in Hinduism. The dalits, treated as untouchables, and women did not have right to *moksha*. They were also denied economic opportunities.
13. Bal Gangadhar Tilak wrote this book during his six-year imprisonment in the prison of Mandalay (Myanmar) between 1908–1914. The book was published in 1915. It is a critique of the most sacred scripture of Hinduism, *Bhagvad Gita*. There are three paths to liberation from the cycle of birth and death in Hinduism, *Gyan Marg* (the path of knowledge about God and creation), *Bhakti Marg* (devoting oneself to God, emphasizing sentiments instead of knowledge), and *Karma Marg*, which means a person should do his duty uprightly without caring for outcome. Tilak argues that *Gita* preached *Karma Marg*. He exhorted Hindus to realize their duty towards their nation and participate in the struggle for independence.
14. Quoted in Louis Fischer, *Gandhi: His Life and Message for the World*, New York: New American Library, 1960, p. 49.

Masculinity in the Guaraní Religious Tradition

ANGÉLICA OTAZÚ

This text addresses the idea of masculinity in indigenous religious tradition, particularly the Guaraní, a condition inferred from some cultural manifestations and expressions, such as the assignment of roles in daily activities and characteristics of the Guaraní language. The studies carried out in the Guaraní culture and the testimonies collected in some indigenous communities are analysed. The main characteristics around masculinity are established, except that the perspective of ancestral practice is uncertain, due to the precarious socio-economic situation of the actors in question.

I Introduction

This text explains the idea of masculinity in the Latin American indigenous religious tradition, centred on the Guaraní culture, since in this region there are a multitude of people with these language(s) and culture. The territory of the Guaraní people covered a large part of the Río de la Plata, probably for 2000 years, and it is estimated that they have emigrated from the Amazon basin, to the subtropical forests of Alto Paraná, Paraguay and Uruguay.

The idea of masculinity can be deduced from some cultural manifestations, such as the assignment of roles to women and men for the performance of daily activities, and the way of speaking. In this culture, normally, the role of each is respected. The main sources are the ethnographic and anthropological studies of the Guaraní culture and the testimonies collected among the indigenous; and because of the complexity of this subject, only some aspects of this culture will be covered, in order to detect a reference that brings us closer to authentic identity and what moves them to act in this way, as well as the arguments for the Guaraní way of being.

In this context, the questions that guide our work will be: What is the cultural expression that most appropriately reflects the idea of masculinity? What are the fundamentals of the roles assigned according to each gender? What is the role of religiosity in the sexual division of labour? What is the perspective on tradition and ancestral practice, under current social, economic, and political pressure?

To delve into the subject, the characteristics of the Guaraní language are a good starting point to inquire into and deepen the customs of this people. The Guaraní language has the particularity of having a vocabulary specific to women and men and also has a common family vocabulary. Logically, cultural expression allows us to decipher how they understand themselves and their relationship with other living beings. For this we will establish several examples, which accurately describe what we have been asserting.

The intentionality of this differentiation will be difficult to determine, however, it suggests that cultural distinguishes the roles of people of both sexes and that this tradition would be long-standing, since it has a broad kinship vocabulary. Communication, primarily oral, is another characteristic of the Guaraní language, which reinforces the transmission from generation to generation to dynamize experience and tradition.

The nomenclature of kinship is another way of access to culture, which constitutes a singular richness. It explains not only masculinity and femininity but also the development of the language and the capacity for oral expression of the people, at the same time, it imprints the wisdom of the people and their society. It describes the internal structure of the organization of the Guaraní nation. We present below, the aspects considered determinant in the conception of masculinity in the aforementioned culture, the imprint of religiosity on the idea of gender, the sexual division of labour, clothing, and the characteristics of the Tupí-Guaraní linguistic family.

II Cultural aspects that determine masculinity

To understand the life and behaviour of the Guaraní, it is essential to know their history, their tradition, and social organization. In that context, the notion of masculinity is an important cultural factor, which is perceived from two fundamental aspects: on the one hand, in the names of kinship and on the other hand, in the sexual division of labour, the role that each one plays in community. The other forms of generic distinction derive from the mentioned aspects. The social organization is essentially based on the connection with religiosity; for that reason, the religious role assigned according to gender awards it a religious meaning and foundation. Therefore, the lack of compliance would mean a challenge to their spirituality and belief. The consequences could be serious; they believe in the possibility of receiving punishment, both physically and morally. As much disease as the lack of success in entrepreneurial activities. According to the statements of the elders, disobedience or alteration of roles, in the worst case, could even cause the death of a loved one.

It is necessary to mention, in addition, that in times past clothing would not have played a preponderant role in the distinction of gender. This statement follows from the characteristics of the area where they lived. It is known that the traditional territory of the Guaraní has a subtropical climate, where warm temperatures are present almost throughout the year and generally, due to the intense humidity, the indigenous preferred to walk almost naked and wear body paintings extracted from the urucu fruit to protect against insects. Then there is a high probability that the current clothing comes from other cultures, usually from the European.

From the campaign of the conquest and the evangelizing mission of the colonial stage, the indigenous would have been forced to wear a garment to cover their bodies, and obviously, the adopted the Spanish-style outfits. In this way, women learned to wear skirts and men pants and shirts. However, there is a certain type of clothing that the Kaiowá Guaraní already consider their own and traditional, such as the so-called ponchito (poncho), a garment probably introduced by the Spanish, although the name comes from another Amerindian language.[1] There are studies concerning traditional indigenous clothing, which managed to identify the names, describe the measurements and the use of a variety of clothes. Among them are three main men's garments, which were part of the traditional clothing of the Kaiowá: the chiripá, the chumbé, and the ponchito.[2]

98

As for the current situation, one observes in the Kaiowá Guaraní communities that there is a collective cooperation for resistance and survival. What is most pressing today is the recovery of their ancestral territories and sacred sites, which by right are theirs. While there are mostly male leaders in the communities, there are also some female leaders. Men and women manage to work in coordination to overcome constant external conflicts both in Mato Grosso do Sul, Brazil and in Amambay, Paraguay. They seek the support of organizations, study in schools, colleges and universities, and are dedicated to their teaching, to move their people forward and preserve their identity.

III Their religiosity

The Guaraní people are known for their mysticism and religiosity, each person has their own prayer and takes it to the end of their life. Their philosophy of life is marked by spiritual experience. To such an extent, it could be said that this culture is clearly governed by norms of a religious nature, and as such, its behaviours obey those norms. For the same reason, children and young people are taught to learn and experience spirituality, to find their own word; to respect and honour religious guidelines. "The Guaraní religion is a religion of the inspired word."[3] According to the myth of the creation of the Mbyá-Guaraní, the word *Ñe'ẽ* is the soul, sent to earth by *Ñande Ru Tenonde*[4] to be incorporated into the creature that will be born:

> "When a being is about to take a seat [be born] a being that rejoices with those who wear the badge of masculinity, the emblem of femininity, sends a good soul-word to earth to be incarnated", said Our First Father to the true Fathers of the soul-words of their children.[5]

In Mbyá-Guaraní *jeguaka* means man; masculine humanity. There exists, in addition, a religious self-designation of the Mbyá, that is expressed in their language, *jeguakáva porãngue i*[6] (those who wear the badge of masculinity).

Likewise, the Kaiowá Guaraní and Pãi Tavyterã value participation in the rites, principally, the kunumi pepy (sacred initiation of the men consisting in the perforating of the lower lip). This rite signifies the presentation and incorporation of boys, into society, and during the ceremony the tembeta is placed on the lower lip, which symbolizes maturity. A ceremony which includes only the men. The candidate receives instructions on his role in the community, and this is the moment of the symbolic passing from childhood to puberty.

> With the initiation of boys, there is a collective ceremony that represents the rise of a new age group to the category of puberty, it arouses the interest of the whole community. Yet that of a girl is an individual event, and for this very reason its social reach is much more restricted, which is why the ceremonial apparatus is considered unnecessary. Furthermore, it can be said that the Guaraní culture is markedly male oriented. Religion is, not exclusively, but predominantly in the hands of men, and it is through them that the dominant aspects of the cultural ethos are expressed in a more clear and sensitive way. It is understandable, therefore, that events related to the male world deserve greater participation or social interest, among them the initiation of boys – although as we saw earlier, there is (from a social and cultural point of view) no strict division between age groups.[7]

The anthropologist Egon Schaden considered that the Guaraní culture is male-oriented, however, he also admits that religion is not only in the hands of males, even if they are the ones who dominate and direct it officially. It can be observed, for example, during the ritual celebrations that the leader is a male, he is the one who gives the sermon to the community or parental group. Women, meanwhile, accompany their husbands during the ritual of the *Jeroky ñembo'e* (ritual dance), mark the rhythm with the takua,[8] made of bamboo. In that sense, other students of the Guaraní culture point out that 'Men and women participate equally in religious life, in the education of children, in medicine and in institutionalized social life.[9]

In any case, one might think that the core of religious experience and the practice of rites, does not reside in a hierarchical structure, but rather in the participation of all members of the community, beginning with the ritual dance, which is circular. In addition, there are communities led politically and spiritually by women. In some cases the wives of the male leaders inherit the power of their husbands, after being widowed, and are respected and accepted as leaders.

Now, we admit that from contact with western culture, leadership itself has been transforming. Its validity, of course, will depend on many factors, both public policies and the perseverance and conviction of the new generations. It will require a lot of effort to protect natural resources, and on the other hand, a lot of strength to follow the ancestral religious traditions, which are linked to the care of the land, water resources, fauna and flora, in short, the planet itself. Obviously, they have a strong will to continue fighting for a space to practice their traditional customs; they even use new technologies to publicize their cultural expressions. They also urge the authorities to value and respect their way of being, and prioritize the preservation of their identity as a people.

It is known that for the Guaraní every inch of the earth is sacred. They understand that there is no territory without living beings, and that the same territory is an organism. They ask mother earth for permission for any activity that could alter her ecosystem, with singing to the rhythm of the circular dance. With this they symbolize that man does not dominate the earth, nor does man have the liberty to harm nature. Religion is their philosophy of life, their mysticism is to respect nature, their ethics of reciprocity and the word *Ñe'ẽ* is sacred. When they are displaced or evicted, their very spirituality disintegrates.

They practice the community of material and spiritual goods. Happiness resides in sharing, that all can enjoy good living, in harmony with nature. Christian theologians could learn from the Guaraní religious universe to live with nature, in this way, to better attune with the daily life of the people and the Church, to move from theory to praxis. To share a little more studies and reflection with those who need it and with the simplest. Above all, to know how to dance with the rhythm of the signs of the times.

IV Sexual division of labour

In Guaraní culture, the community has a distribution of tasks based on the sexual division of labour, because there are well-defined tasks, reserved only for men or only for women. In that sense, traditionally, it is the man who supports the family with his work from the farm and other chores. The Paĩ Tavyterã carry out various types of activities, and they clearly distinguish which are proper to men and to women; according to the

research of contemporary anthropologists:
> Men are in charge of heavy work on the farm (cutting trees, burning, weeding, hoeing), they plant avati tupi (tupi corn), pakova (banana), mamóne (papaya), rice, petỹ (tobacco), and use machinery. They go hunting, look for honey, ka'a (yerba mate), and firewood and are responsible for the pigpens, fences, corral ropes, carts, care of older domestic animals and building houses. They also make bows and arrows, baskets, yrupẽ (lattices), karaguata weaving, mimby (flute), mbaraka (maraca, rattle), apyka (bench), kaguĩ ryru (chicha glass), angu'a (mortar), avati soka (mallet), etc.[10]

The women, on the other hand, take care of the home and the children, apart from also collaborating in the planting of white corn and the collection of wild fruits and honey, they are dedicated to the making of handicrafts, among other activities. Women, in today's Paĩ communities, 'are responsible for the production of ceramics and textiles and plant avati morotĩ (white corn), jety (sweet potato), kara (a tuber), etc.'[11] However, it is also recognized that there is co-responsibility for some activities, where men and women interact, for example, both 'fish, sew clothes, plant kumanda (bean), mandi'o (manioc) and takuare'ẽ (sweet cane), collect wild fruits and ..., carry loads, cook and care for domestic animals such as pigs, chickens, and ducks [...].'.[12] In this way, one could say there is a balance in the tasks of the home.

The respective roles are observed and assumed thanks to a mechanism, that the community exercises over its members; therefore, it employs strict controls to preserve and energize this tradition. The members learn to respect the role of each, obviously, without entering into conflict or a rivalry, that is, the corresponding roles are not objects of questioning, since there is no dispute on the issue. Men do not participate in activities stereotyped to be women's.

The control mechanisms are obtained, through prohibitions that are implicitly in the sayings and beliefs of each community such as the *mbora'u*, omen. Likewise, they are encouraged in the shaman's sermons and are energized in conversations and daily life between parents and children; they are normally transmitted orally from generation to generation. One also learns with daily life and the testimony of adults.

There are anecdotes, that the elders commonly tell the younger, in order to make known and promote ancestral customs, while discovering their own identity and understanding the importance of belonging to the community. Thus, transfers of the structure of culture and tradition are part of the education of children and youth. It is the way of guarding through the formation of the identity of the population and projecting the future of the community.

V Traditional medicine

Those empower to heal ailments, usually are religious leaders, shamans. Still today in the communities there are people who go to the shamans in search of relief from pain. The healing rite consists of prayer and singing, and in some case, a home remedy or natural medicine is recommended for patients who they approach, confident of being able to heal. The method of health care includes affection, the closeness of loved ones, the prayer and singing of the entire community, which is usually led by a *rezador* (female healer). Recovery is considered to require the patient's attention and good rest. There are certain diseases that are attributed to the intervention of some spirit or malevolence; and to scare this away they need to redouble the prayer and practice different rites.

On the other hand, it should be noted that the Guaraní dominated the jungle and have demonstrated this by their ability to classify plants; they also know the healing properties of each species. The plants that are fit for health, for the treatment of diseases and convalescence, but also they distinguish those that are toxic.

The art of healing with natural remedies and the selection of herbalism constitute an ancient wisdom, and it is has also been asserted that the Tupi-Guaraní linguistic family is one that contributed the most names to botany after Greek and Latin. Likewise, the role of healers is recovered in the strengthening of spiritual life.

VI Characteristics of language

Regarding the use of language, it is found that both men and woman have their own vocabulary, which they acquire with experience and living in community. We can indicate that in the past, there was even a way of saying yes, different for both sexes, in this way, men said *ta* and women said *hẽe*. Thus the word ta was recorded as an entry in the dictionary of the Guaraní language: 'ta, yes – says the male granting-." [13] Ta means yes and is used by the male when he grants something, whose use has been lost over time, and 'hẽe, yes (granting) says the woman',[14] today hẽe is universally used.

It is worth emphasizing that the Guaraní language does not have gender, and therefore, there is a specific vocabulary, whose function is to distinguish the male and female sex from the speakers. The way to name the descendants of both is also different. The following table shows what has been found:

Kuimba'énte he'íva: Exclusively masculine use	Kuñánte he'íva: Exclusively feminine use
Tajýra-rajy: daughter	Memby: son or daughter
Ta'ýra - ra'y: son	Memby kuña: daughter
Tajýra - rajy ranga: goddaughter and stepdaughter	Memby ranga: godson and stepchild
Ta'ýra - ra'y ranga: godson and stepson	Memby kuimba'e: son
Tembireko(Osc.): wife	Ména: husband
Tembirekorã: girlfriend/fiancee	Menarã: boyfriend/fiancé
Teindýra - reindy: sister	Tykéra - ryke: older sister
Tyke'ýra - ryke'y: older brother	Kypy'y: younger sister
Tyvýra - ryvy: younger brother	Kyvy: brother

This particularity of the Guaraní language and culture was detected and registered by missionaries in the colonial era and published in 1640 in Madrid, specifically, in the Catechism of the Guaraní language of Antonio Ruiz de Montoya. Although said registration was made within the evangelizing project, with the interest of identifying the line of kinship among the Guaraní. That is, with the desire to propagate and implement the teaching of the sacrament of marriage, mentioned in Guaraní. However, today it is an important document that facilitates the study of understanding of the kinship system of the Guaraní of the pre-Hispanic era. It even figure among one of the few sources to explore the anthropological dimension of peoples before contact with European colonizers.

The nomenclature of kinship in the Guaraní culture describes the relationship between family members; and allows one to recognize the degree of kinship, for example, uncle and aunt, will depend on the degree of kinship of each one, and if it is the older or younger brother of his father. Each of the uncles receives a different name, as well as from the mother. Similarly, in the specific nomenclature there are expressions to refer to fraternal bonds.

In Ruiz de Montoya (1640),[15] the expressions referring to first-degree relatives among siblings were recorded, the male says: *che ryke'y*, my older brother; *che ryvy*, my younger brother; *y che reindy*, my sister. There are also specific names for political relatives, brothers-in-law, and sisters-in-law. In the same way, it happens with the female vocabulary.

Naturally, this kinship system is still in force and family vocabulary is used, to a large extent, still today, in the various communities, as well as among Paraguayan Guaraní speakers, despite contact and co-existence with other different cultures and languages. Precisely, family vocabulary is closely linked to the identity of the people, therefore, it is an integral part of their cultural heritage. They strive to transmit, revitalize, and disseminate it as a true treasure in their communities.

VII In conclusion

Masculinity is noticeable in different manifestations of Guaraní culture. A more detailed analysis requires a multidisciplinary approach. Likewise, it is necessary to analyse from the perspective of the native peoples, how they manage to forge their tradition in the face of the vicissitudes of the present times. The neglect/harm has accelerated for more than four decades, due to deforestation and mechanized agriculture that increasingly extends to their Tekoha, sacred territories. Although the indigenous have an interest in preserving and energizing their culture, it is difficult to know how much more they can withstand the forced separations of the communities. To ensure their well-being, the current national laws that protect indigenous people must be applied. So they can live according to their traditional patters in their own territory, where they create and recreate their culture and language. We could learn from them to protect and save the planet, for the good of all humanity.

Translated by Thia Cooper

Notes

1. The word 'poncho' comes from mapudungun, pontro (wool or woll cloth); http://etimologias.dechile.net/?poncho.
2. On txiripá, or txumbé, and ponchito, see Egon Schaden, *Aspectos Fundamentais da cultura guarani*, 3a. ed., São Paulo, EPU: Universidade de São Paulo, 1974, p. 31.
3. Meliá, *El guaraní*, p. 42. [All quotations translated by this article's translator.]
4. Our First Father.
5. Leon Cadogan, *Ayvu Rapyta: Textos Míticos de los Mbyá-Guaraní del Guairá*, 3rd. ed., Asunción, CEADUC-CEPAG. 1997, p. 67.
6. Ver Leon Cadogan, *Diccionario Mbyá-Guaraní Castellano*, Asunción: CEADUC-CEPAG, 1992, p. 67.
7. Schaden, *Aspectos Fundamentais*, p. 85.
8. A native instrument made of bamboo.
9. Bartomeu Melià and Friedl Grünberg, *Los Pãi Tavyterã: Etnografía guaraní del Paraguay contemporáneo*, Asunción: CEPAG – CEADUC, 2008, p. 113.
10. Melià and Grünberg, *Los Pãi Tavyterã*, pp. 112–113.
11. Melià and Grünberg, *Los Pãi Tavyterã*, p. 113.
12. Melià and Grünberg, *Los Pãi Tavyterã*, p. 113.
13. Antonio Ruiz de Montoya, *Tesoro de la lengua Guaraní* (Madrid, 1639), Leipzig: W. Drugulin, 1876, p. 347.
14. Ruiz de Montoya, *Tesoro*, 1876, p. 149.
15. Antonio Ruiz de Montoya. *Catecismo de la lengua Guaraní* (Madrid, 1640), Leipzig: W. Drugulin, 1876, pp. 324–32.

Part Three: Masculinities and/in the Catholic Church

Essentially Different Men?
Varieties of Clerical Masculinity

THERESIA HEIMERL

The public regards clerical masculinity as a 'different sort' of masculinity, and this can also be seen in its media portrayals. This article investigates the historical origin and development of clerical masculinity from early Christianity to the present. Part II analyses the justification in systematic theology of the 'otherness' of clerical masculinity, using as a basis the documents of the Second Vatican Council. Finally the article asks what effects the particular definition of clerical masculinity has, and whether it can survive in the conditions of our time.

I Introduction

'A priest is not a man. He is something less… or something more. It depends.' This observation is made by Flora, the young revolutionary woman and niece of the famous village priest from the last book of Giovanni Guareschi's *Don Camillo* series, published in 1969. Guareschi's books present an ideal type of the clerical man, and the film versions preserve it to precisely the last point in history when it still had validity.

Almost fifty years later clerical masculinity is only really authentic as a stylised artistic device. An example is the speeded-up scene from the television series *The Young Pope* in which director Paolo Sorrentino has his Pius XIII choose his brocade shoes and ceremonial attire, and put on his sunglasses and tiara, before he is carried into the Sistine Chapel on the *sedia gestatoria* to the song *I'm sexy and I know it*.[2]

The Catholic priest as a particular form of masculinity is so firmly rooted in the cultural memory of the Western world that his image is employed even today in mass media productions, including commercials.[3] The dark shadow of the concerned, selfless, shrewd – and heterosexually attractive – cleric of cinema and TV is the money-grubbing, corrupt, stupid, paedophile priest; he is also among the stock characters of media masculinities as a particular form. The fictional clerics reflect in sharp focus the real special status – positive or negative – that clerics still possess in conversations in the Western world.

This article seeks to investigate this particular form of masculinity and sketch its significance and problems for the interpretation of masculinity in general. First it looks at the historical origin and development of the cleric as an alternative type of masculinity in the context of the origin and spread of the Church. Second, it analyses the characteristics attributed to this by the Church's official teaching, which even today define the cleric and his masculinity, and discusses their interaction with Church structures. The conclusion offers some reflections on clerical masculinity in current discussions of masculinity and problem areas in the Church.

II A short history of the cleric as a 'special' man
A look at the historical origin of the cleric is a look at the origin and development of Christianity in the first centuries.[4] The term itself, derived from the Greek, originally meant an office-holder chosen by lot, and it was not until the beginning of the 3rd century that it developed the meaning of a specific 'class' of holders of ecclesiastical offices such bishop, presbyter or deacon, though offices such as reader, sub-deacon and exorcist are often included among the clergy. In the society of the Roman empire they formed a particular social group, which since the time of Emperor Constantine enjoyed the same privileges as the officials conducting the worship of the Roman gods. As Peter Brown's latest study has shown in detail,[5] until the fall of the Roman empire the majority of the members of this group thought of themselves as a social group with specific privileges and duties, but not necessarily as an elite with an 'alternative' way of life or masculinity – the majority of clerics were married, had families in the ancient sense and were a part of the complex social structure of the late Roman empire.[6]

The status of this 'different sort' of man, which stood in sharp contrast to the inherited constructions of Roman masculinity, was the project of a numerically small elite. This elite, which included in its number such well-known figures such as Ambrose, Jerome, and Augustine, but also Paulinus of Nola, Cassian and others, used their writings to spread the still influential idea of the special man in the service of God. The main inspiration for this idea was the ascetic, in the form that this figure first appeared in the eastern Mediterranean, a man who renounced all worldly pleasure and obligation and lived in the desert alone or in community and devoted himself entirely to God. A key part of this radical way of life was renunciation of sexuality, on the one hand as a renunciation of social obligations such as marriage and family, but also as a return to a state like paradise before the fall. Peter Brown describes these men, and their imitators in the West, very vividly as pale, unwashed creatures, in deliberate contrast to the groomed and totally trained Roman nobles – which made the contrast even greater, since the most influential propagandists of this new ideal had once belonged to this upper class.[7] Originally these ascetics in the desert were not clerics at all, in the sense of men with offices in social structures. However, the most influential theologians of the late empire linked the ministry of the clerics with the strict way of life of the ascetics, first mainly as an ideal, and so created a new elite. In this old masculine virtues such as self-sacrifice, military discipline and leadership qualities were to be raised to a new level by new Christian virtues embodied in the ascetic life. The cleric, as imagined by Ambrose or Augustine, was a heterosexual man who renounced his sexuality and a soldier who placed his body and mind in the service of the Church rather than the military.

This new clerical masculinity proved extremely useful in the following centuries in many ways: the Church had men without family obligations or claims, but they, as a social elite, could set themselves above other powerful men (nobles and even the emperor and kings) and shape the intellectual world, alone for the most part, and at least have a key influence on administration. When Georges Duby talked about a triangle of 'knight, lady and priest',[8] he neatly indicated the two normative structures of masculinity in the West. The middle ages especially show how the new, clerical ideal of masculinity begins to change the 'old' ideal of the fighting and erotically active man. The knights of the epic of courtly love may not be ascetics, but restraint in the service of an adored lady is highly prized, and the eroticism of renunciation and civilised masculinity found in this poetry is essentially the work of clerical authors such as Chrétien de Troyes, one of the creators of the genre.[9] Clerical masculinity is for long periods of history the only literate form of masculinity and the one that has determined discussion of gender and gender roles.

The particular nature of clerical masculinity became even clearer when it was questioned by the reformation. The reformed churches simply abolished the cleric as a consecrated, celibate figure and replaced him by the traditional masculinity of the *paterfamilias*, the father as head of the household.[10] Catholic clerical masculinity was regarded by the reformers as a mistaken development, as a false masculinity, and catholicism as a whole declared a 'feminised' religion.[11] This image of the Catholic cleric as unmanly and 'effeminate',and so implicitly homosexual, remains a part of the discussion about clerics even today. The reformation critique made clerical masculinity an elite form of masculinity in which 'manly' virtues could and should be practised in the service of the Church and so provide rules for the other type of masculinity, whose gender identity was questioned and constantly required justification. The resulting insecurity about clerical masculinity in Catholic discussion down to today will be examined later.

III *Non gradu tantum, sed essentia*: the essential otherness of clerical masculinity

Clerics are distinguished from laity by ordination. According to the Church's official teaching, this is not a mere difference in social status, but an essential difference in the strictest sense of the word; '*essentia et non gradu tantum*' ('in essence and not only in degree'), runs the formula that is still valid and which makes clerics a different sort of people.[12] Or, more precisely, a different sort of men, since ordination is still linked to one gender, the masculine. The formulation, especially in its Latin version, reveals that the cleric, as a construct of systematic theology, goes back to a distant phase of philosophical and theological history, in which talk of *esse et essentia* (being and essence) was a central element of any interpretation of the world. The key change in based on the sacrament, which has an effect over time (*character indelibilis*, an indelible character). This feature of all sacraments leads, in the case of the sacrament of order, to the situation in which belonging to a particular level in the social hierarchy, or what in modern terms we would call a profession, acquires a metaphysical character. The cleric is, not just in performing the various acts of his ministry, but wholly and for ever a different masculine being from all other men. Among the metaphysical aspects of clerical masculinity there is, finally, the *repraesentatio Christi*, the representation of Christ.[13] For this aspect, as opposed to the common priesthood of all believers, gender is constitutive, as is always emphasised in those official Church documents that reject the ordination of women.[14] The masculinity of Jesus and the apostles he chose is stressed as a nature essentially distinguished by gender and regarded as a precondition for the particular 'acting in the person of Christ' by the 'ministerial priesthood', as *Lumen Gentium* calls it.

Today the priest has become a synonym for the clerical man and his essential difference; other canonical statuses such as unordained religious brothers or permanent (often married) deacons are generally no longer associated with the concept of the cleric. They seem to lack the recognisable, emphatic special status of the cleric. This clerical otherness was an is emphasised by an otherness in their practical situation. At the end of the Roman empire most clerics were already living a common life in bishop's residences, monasteries or at Christian shrines.[15] For various reasons, this community life of men is something more than the relatively common philosophical associations familiar since Plato: the status of cleric, once acquired, could not be cancelled; it meant incorporation into the Church structure and being at its service, and these men were under an obligation of sexual abstinence. In other words, clerical masculinity was also a form of collective masculinity. Even where there was no community life, as in the case of secular priests as envisaged by the Council of Trent, it was regarded as important to train for this clerical masculinity in a seminary or, even earlier, in a junior seminary, and the obligatory nature of this special life style was stressed.

Gender was and is essentially constructed through the symbolism of the body, that is, dress, hair style and general bearing. That also applies to clerical masculinity. It was for centuries inscribed 'on the body': the tonsure, originally a sign of the absence of freedom and of repentance, became a visible sign of the cleric even in the lowest degrees, and did not officially lose its status until the 20th century.[16] The discussion about whether the special form of clerical dress is meant to be a sign of wealth or poverty became commonplace as early as Francis of Assisi. Even today dress has the role of an iconic identifier, and the habit as clothing for a monk (whether or not the person in question is a monk or religious) and the black cassock, or at least a black suit, but always the white collar, have become established as denoting a secular priest.[17] In addition bishops and cardinals have purple or red ceremonial robes.

The most striking peculiarity of clerical masculinity, however, is the stress on a clearly heterosexual masculinity alongside a renunciation of the practice of this manly heterosexuality. What can be explained historically, as we have seen, by particular ideas and influences, and by practical structural considerations, on a systematic and psychological level becomes a permanent paradox. Clerical masculinity is not an alternative form of masculinity in the sense of being a break with traditional heteronormativity, but rather its raising to a higher ontological plane through the negation of sexual activity. The discussions about whether men with homosexual tendencies should be allowed to be ordained priests brings into focus exactly this special construction of clerical masculinity.[18] The argument is not simply about renouncing a lived sexuality, which, of course, would apply to any orientation; it is about transcending the similarly fixed heterosexual masculinity. The battle against any form of cultural or historical deconstruction of gender roles, with the discussion of 'gender ideology' in the latest official Vatican documents,[19] exposes the very special clerical variety of insecure masculinity in post-modern times. If gender is something fluid, influenced by social and historical factors, could not clerical masculinity also be one of many alternative interpretations of masculinity, dependent on these factors and not based on a 2000-year old essential difference?

IV Clerical masculinity: present and future

The clerical man as a 'different' sort of man has become a trademark of Catholic Christianity. The question is whether the real clerical men of the 21st century still correspond to the model, and whether they can or want to. Both historically and in systematic theology, until a few decades ago clerical masculinity was always defined in terms of Western traditions and developments. Their definitions were transposed into other continents and cultures without any thought for their gender images. The second or third generation of clerics from these regions, when clerical masculinity has only just become part of their identity, now finds itself confronted with discussions about gender in the Western world that question this identity, and reacts with incomprehension. In his geographical and cultural homeland, meanwhile, the clerical man has within a few decades become an endangered species, whose habitat has been rapidly transformed. In 1989 Eugen Drewermann could still talk about the 'psychogram of the cleric' whose identity had been collectively formed or deformed in an established standard programme.[20] Thirty years later the clerical man as an archetype, as Drewermann described him, hardly exists any longer in the Western world. Alongside the collective formation of clerical masculinity from the beginning of puberty, there are now very different individual paths, often taken by fully adult men, leading to a monastery or seminary. Their image of the cleric is the product of personal experiences and put together from historical images or even fictional images from the media. The obviousness of otherness as a central leadership element of the Christian community has given way to a unique otherness based on an assortment of texts.

The question of how to deal with one's own masculinity, for so long avoided by pious metaphysical rhetoric, emerges with stark clarity in the charge that clerical masculinity is a masculinity that endangers oneself and others: must not a man who is essentially defined by his unexplored sexuality, and through this portrayed as a spiritual leader, inevitably become either a violent sex criminal or an emotional cripple? Is clerical masculinity a particularly treacherous form of toxic masculinity that hides its inability to deal with new gender role models behind a hypocritical façade?

Clerical masculinity is a particular type of masculinity, and a product of history that deserves to be looked at more closely. It made possible discussion about alternative gender roles possible long before secular theories. It demonstrated that masculinity is more than active sexuality and domination of women and children. Clerical masculinity created forms of shared living beyond the family and in this was successful for centuries. Just at the point in history at which the Western world, which none other than these clerical men helped to shape, is beginning to develop ideas of alternative masculinity and life-styles, the model of clerical masculinity is in crisis. One key to a comparison with secular forms of new concepts of masculinity may be the relationship between structure and personal (gender) identity. A form of male identity bound up with demands and restrictions can hardly any longer be a prior condition for a Church office, and certainly not – and this may be the central point – for one's whole life. Identities are fluid, and in more than one direction. The irreversibility of the essential difference of a cleric's existence is frightening: a man, any man, can change and wants to change, to discover new aspects of his own masculinity and abandon old ones (like St Augustine 1600 years ago). And finally we must be allowed to ask whether the particularity, even if it is conceived of as an ontological difference, must absolutely be located in the crypto-Gnostic legacy of sexual abstinence.

In scenes from film and television, abandoning clerical dress is often portrayed as abandoning clerical identity, while conversely putting on clerical dress is presented as a deliberate construction of that identity, as in the scene from *The Young Pope* mentioned at the beginning of this article. The fascinating question these scenes face us with is whether and how much of the cleric is left in the man in ordinary clothes – or even without any clothes. For a reinterpretation of clerical masculinity it might be helpful to modify our initial quotation from 1989: A priest is also a man. He can be something less... or something more. It depends.

Translated by Francis McDonagh

Notes

1. Giovanni Guareschi, *Don Camillo Meets Hell's Angels*, Harmondsworth, 1972, US edition: *Don Camillo Meets the Flower Children*, New York, 1969.
2. HBO, *The Young Pope*, episode 5: https://www.hbo.com/the-young-pope
3. See the anthology edited by Theresia Heimerl und Lisa Kienzl, *Helden in Schwarz: Priester in Film und TV*, Marburg, 2014.
4. For an overview, see Alexandre Faivre, 'Klerus', 'Kleriker', in: *Lexikon für Theologie und Kirche*, vol. 6, 3rd ed., Freiburg, 2006, pp 131–133.
5. Peter Brown, *Through the Eye of a Needle: Wealth, the Fall of Rome and the Making of Christianity in the West*, Princeton, NJ, and Oxford, 2012.
6. See especially Peter Brown, *Through the Eye of a Needle*, pp 241-258.
7. See Brown, pp 220-221.

8. Georges Duby, *The Knight, The Lady, and the Priest: The Making of Modern Marriage in Medieval France*, Harmondsworth, 1985, and Chicago IL, 1993.

9. Cf Jacques Le Goff, *The Birth of Europe*, Malden, MA, and Oxford, 2005, p. 136.

10. See Albrecht Koschorke, *Die Heilige Familie und ihre Folgen*, Frankfurt, 2000, pp 146–157.

11. See Bernard Schneider, 'Gesucht: Der katholische Mann: Die katholische Kirche in Deutschland und die Männerwelt im 19. und 20. Jahrhundert', *Trierer Theologische Zeitschrift*, 2 (2014), 85–109.

12. Vatican II, *Lumen Gentium* 10.2: http://www.vatican.va/archive/hist_councils/ii_vatican_council/documents/vat-ii_const_19641121_lumen-gentium_en.html

13. *Lumen Gentium* 10.2: 'acting in the person of Christ'.

14. See Congregation for the Doctrine of the Faith, *Inter Insigniores* (1976): http://www.vatican.va/roman_curia/congregations/cfaith/documents/rc_con_cfaith_doc_19761015_inter-insigniores_en.html; John Paul II, *Ordinatio Sacerdotalis* (1994): http://www.vatican.va/content/john-paul-ii/en/apost_letters/1994/documents/hf_jp-ii_apl_19940522_ordinatio-sacerdotalis.html

15. Brown, *Through the Eye of a Needle*, cites the examples of Paulinus of Nola (pp 224-240) and Augustine (pp 173-184).

16. See Hubertus Lutterbach, Article 'Tonsur', in *Lexikon für Theologie und Kirche*, vol. 10, 3rd ed., Freiburg, 2006, 107–108.

17. Theresia Heimerl and Lisa Kienzl, 'Kirchentreuer Humor: Priester in Komödien', in: Theresia Heimerl and Lisa Kienzl (ed.), *Helden in Schwarz: Priester in Film und TV*, Marburg, 2014, pp 138–141.

18. Congregation for Catholic Education, *Instruction Concerning the Criteria for the Discernment of Vocations with regard to Persons with Homosexual Tendencies in view of their Admission to the Seminary and to Holy Orders* (2005): http://www.vatican.va/roman_curia/congregations/ccatheduc/documents/rc_con_ccatheduc_doc_20051104_istruzione_en.html

19. Congregation for Catholic Education, *Male and Female He Created Them* (2019): http://www.vatican.va/roman_curia/congregations/ccatheduc/documents/rc_con_ccatheduc_doc_20190202_maschio-e-femmina_en.pdf

20. Eugen Drewermann, *Kleriker: Psychogramm eines Ideals*, Olten, 1989.

Masculinity and Sexual Abuse in the Church

JULIE HANLON RUBIO

The sexual abuse crisis in the Catholic church which was reignited in the summer of 2017 has rightly led to calls for lament, justice for victims, self-examination, and structural change. Many theories about root causes have been advanced, but most are not supported by the social science on sexual abuse. Given that men are the primary perpetrators of abuse of both adults and children, the most significant root cause could be masculinity. This essay uses contemporary research on gender as a lens through which to read analyses of clergy sexual abuse and cover-up. I argue that because the clergy sexual abuse is gendered at every level, transformation requires attention to problematic conceptions and performances of masculinity.

I Introduction

As a Catholic lay woman who forms priests alongside lay men and women for ecclesial ministry, I have experienced the latest round of revelations of clergy sexual abuse from a unique vantage point. The week I arrived to begin my new job at the Jesuit School of Theology in Berkeley, California, the Pennsylvania Grand Jury report was released. Six months earlier when I interviewed for the job, I had presented a paper on intersections between the #MeToo movement and the emerging #ChurchToo movement. The year has been marked by events related to the scandal: the first heart wrenching conversation at our faculty retreat in August; our school's day of lament and prayer in September; an emotional town hall meeting at a local parish; talks and panels at universities across the country; the release of lists of credibly accused Jesuits (including a priest that had been a SLU

118

colleague and close friend of my family from childhood). It has been a difficult year to be Catholic, even for those who have long histories of being in a complicated relationship with the church. But this year has also brought me closer to priesthood than I have ever been in my life, and I cannot deny that the young scholastics who will soon be ordained fill me with hope.

In this context of despair and hope, I delved deeper into research on clergy sexual abuse, and it became clear to me that all of the most popular explanations lacked the gender analysis which is indispensable to understanding both abuse and its cover-up. The conservative narrative stresses the need for priests to recommit to sexual purity so they might better enact their roles as fathers or shepherds. The liberal narrative stresses the problematic nature of celibacy and, often, the priesthood itself. The moderate narrative privileges accountability and transparency as antidotes to clericalism. I argue that because clergy sexual abuse is gendered, transformation requires attention to how problematic conceptions of masculinity deform the relationships of celibates just as those of non-celibates. I will move through the argument in three parts: gender as a lens for understanding sexual violence, clergy sexual abuse as inextricably tied to masculinity, and 'undoing masculinity' as a practice of resistance to an ecclesial culture that enables abuse.

II Gender as a lens for understanding sexual violence

Questions about gender which have occupied theorists since the 1990s have only recently been taken up by Catholic theologians, so to use gender as a lens to consider clergy sexual abuse will require going beyond existing lines of analysis. As Judith Butler notes, feminist thinkers originally distinguished biological sex (male and female) from gendered expression (masculine and feminine) and focused on gender discrimination, but now gender has come to signify an embodied identity with a complex mix of biological, social, and psychological sources and varied performances, and gender-based violence targets a broad spectrum of those who transgress the binary.[1] The Catholic tradition is struggling to catch up.

Feminist theologians are leading the way by criticizing gender ideals that limit what women and men can do, but few have engaged the more complex questions of gender theory. Most embrace greater distinction between sex and gender, affirm the existence of diverse sexual orientations, and object to complementarity as well as 'feminine genius'. Some have substantively engaged French post-modernist feminist theorists to argue both for some enduring feminine and masculine characteristics and for diverse gender expressions. Womanist, Latinx, African, and Asian theologians assume and build upon early feminist distinctions between sex and gender and employ gender (along with race, class, etc.) to analyze a range of issues. There is broad acceptance of feminist theorists' claims about the (partial) social construction of gender, gender and power, and sexism, along with attention to sexual violence understood as an act of power.

However, gender theorists have gone much further. Over three decades ago, Butler argued that gender is not simply socially constructed but constituted by 'the stylized repetition of acts through time', or culturally specific performance.[2] A woman or man walks into a feminine or masculine identity as an actor walks onto a stage, with a script, props, a director, a voice coach, and a costume designer. Each actor interprets an existing role in his or her own way, but 'the gendered body acts its part in a culturally restricted corporeal space and enacts interpretations within the confines of already existing directives'.[3] In *Gender Trouble*, Butler essentially dissolves the distinction between sex and gender, musing, 'perhaps it was always already gender' and claiming 'the body in itself is itself a construction', noting with enthusiasm new 'possibilities for agency'.[4] If sex was once assumed to be biological but is, we now know, more complicated to determine, gender becomes the more fundamental category, not simply an expression of sex but an identity one practices, embodies, and reinterprets.[5]

Understanding gender as ongoing performance seems particularly important for analysing sexual violence and clergy sexual abuse in particular. In order to resist it, we have to first understand it as a gendered phenomenon. But most analysts of the crisis are not talking about gender.

III Clergy sexual abuse as gendered
Often those viewing the problem of clergy sexual abuse map their larger concerns onto the issue, blaming homosexuality, the liberalizing trends of the 1960s, celibacy, or priesthood.[6] Yet, though data on clergy sexual abuse is frustratingly limited, these explanations do not hold up. Sexual

abuse, including the abuse of children and teens, is all too common, not just in the U.S. or Europe, but everywhere in the world, especially in schools, families, and other institutions where adults have access to children. Those who are gay, celibate, or priests are not more likely to abuse minors; the vast majority of abusers are heterosexual, non-celibate, and non-priests.[7] Very little is known about the extent and causes of sexual abuse in religions other than Catholicism, but existing research does not suggest that abuse is less common in other faith-based institutions.[8] While the 1960s saw both liberalizing mores and a rise in criminal behaviour of all kinds, it is difficult to establish causal connections between these broad social changes and the relatively small percentage of men who did abuse minors or to explain why women who lived through the same decade did not. Historically, it is much more likely that abuse was unrecognised and under-reported, rather than uncommon.[9] Neither conservative nor liberal theories are supported by the social science literature on sexual violence.

Yet that literature is itself complicated. It is much easier to say what is not true than what it true about sexual abuse. Criminal justice expert Karen Terry examined multiple different explanatory paradigms for sexual offending, and concluded that while some evidence exists for each, it is difficult to argue for one over the other.[10] Research is mostly limited to small populations in mental health institutions or prisons. No one factor (including having been abused or possessing a particular psychological pathology or mental illness) can fully explain the problem. Only five percent of perpetrators can be classified as paedophiles. Attempts to identify factors that set other abusers apart have been unsuccessful, making screening out those likely to abuse nearly impossible.

One factor is not complicated at all: gender is the strongest predictor of who will engage in sexual violence with adults and children, so understanding why men abuse and how abuse is gendered is essential.[11] Feminist scholars, including theologians, have long understood sexual violence as part of the web of sexism that empowers men and dis-empowers women, even those who are not perpetrators or victims. They understand rape primarily as an act of power, rather than sex. Power is surely at work in sexual violence, since the acts revealed, for example, in the Pennsylvania Grand Jury report, map much less easily onto a sexual language of mutuality and intimacy than violation and control.

Perpetrators say not 'I give myself just as I am' or 'I receive and cherish you', but 'I demand that you do this to me' or 'I will do this to you because I can whether you agree or not'. This is power taken and enforced through sexual acts.

Still, power alone may be too simple of an explanation, especially if masculinity is understood as gender performance established through repeated actions. Anne Cossins shows how this framework makes sense of sexual offenders' own narratives in ways most studies focusing on individual characteristics simply cannot.[12] She employs a theory of power and powerlessness to show that perpetrators of child sexual abuse often seek power over vulnerable teens or children as a way of performing masculinity when other avenues are closed to them.[13] This theory coheres both with findings that males who feel their masculinity is threatened are more likely to engage in sexual violence and with those studies showing how powerful men can enact entitlement through sexual dominance.[14]

Focusing on masculinity allows for integration of feminist theories of structural causes of violence with pastoral studies of sex offenders which link poor psychosexual integration, stress, poor boundary setting, and lack of intimacy to abuse.[15] It becomes possible to ask: *why* are male offenders stressed, lacking in intimacy, and bereft of support? *Why* do they find it difficult to set boundaries? Why do few women who may also be isolated or stressed engage in sexual abuse? How might clergy be especially vulnerable, not simply as pastors but *as males*?[16] Their masculinity is linked to a male saviour and a God primarily imaged as male, and it is the justification for their power to preach, preside, and decide. Yet many of their daily tasks might be perceived as feminine and they are not able to engage in the sexual activity that is central to the performance of masculinity for most men. Might clergy sexual abuse be an extreme way of enacting masculinity from spaces of perceived powerlessness and spaces of excess entitlement?

The masculinity lens is helpful even though the majority of clergy sexual abuse of minors is same sex abuse. In male-female sexual violence, male power and privilege (as well as its flip-side, female internalized pressure to give in and remain silent) are central. But this kind of dynamic can also be seen in encounters between same sex adults. Abuse by an adult of a child, whether same or different sex, is similarly gendered, because cultural scripts of masculinity exert power over the imagination in ways that transcend sex. Paradoxically, because children and teens are perceived as more feminine, because they are less powerful and less likely to articulate their sexual desires, sex with them becomes a way of enacting masculinity, regardless of gender.[17]

Gender performance of masculinity need not be sinister. Research on sexual abuse shows that clergy perpetrators gain powers of trust, accessibility, and a presumption of moral blamelessness which allow them to violate boundaries with females in their congregations.[18] Diana Garland argues that even in 'consensual' relationships between male clergy and adult women, sexual activity should never be labelled 'an affair' because people with authority over others are always abusing their power when they cross sexual boundaries. In her extensive research, Garland found that clergy sexual misconduct was common. Perpetrators are so blinded by their privilege that they are unable to experience empathy for their victims, and their sense of entitlement leads them to expect deference. Victims give the deference they think they owe and are unable to critically assess what is being done to them. While this research may seem less relevant to Catholic contexts, recent studies fail to include adult victims, many of whom are likely to be female. Worldwide, clergy sexual abuse may well include a greater proportion of women, as recent allegations from women religious in India, Vietnam, and Philippines show. In all of these contexts, masculinity is performed via grooming and persuasion versus brute force.

The cover-up of abuse can also be understood as gendered performance. When male clergy choose secrecy over exposure, they are protecting male spaces of knowledge and power. Frederic Martel's recent book claiming to pull back the curtain on gay sexual activity in the Vatican may be salacious and lacking in hard evidence, but most reviewers found it difficult to dispute its portrait of the inner-workings of networks that hid male sexual secrets to protect male power.[19] Moreover, though all U.S. bishops were aware of the clergy sexual abuse problem by 1980s and committed to the principles outlined in the *Charter for the Protection of Children and Young People*, the John Jay Report found that implementation of new protocols was inconsistent because the bishops were so committed to tightly controlling information.[20] Though things have improved since the protocols established in Dallas in 2002, according to whistleblower and canon lawyer Jennifer Haselberger, accountability and transparency are far from normative because male clergy have not been willing to yield power to others.[21] Just as networks enable men in entertainment, sports, and politics to protect male power and privilege while disadvantaging their female colleagues, clerical networks protect men who abuse both minors and adults.

IV Undoing gender as a practice of resistance

As important as the push for accountability and transparency in response to abuse and cover-up are, a complex gender analysis suggests that policy change alone is insufficient. In *Undoing Gender*, Butler responds to critics who worry that her gender theory does not provide sufficient grounding for social change, arguing that writing disruptive gender theory is a political act, in keeping with feminism's goal of 'social transformation of gender relations'.[22] Working toward change entails asking questions about survival (e.g., 'Whose life is counted as a life? Whose prerogative is it to live?'). Rather than defining new gender norms to aim for, she offers the example of drag shows as political acts, that 'undo' gender by 'showing us how contemporary notions of reality can be questioned, and new modes of reality instituted'.[23]

What would it mean to 'undo' masculinity in Catholic responses to clergy sexual abuse? Any sort of 'undoing' will require change in individuals and communities, in their understandings of themselves and their desires. In this sense, Pope Francis seems right in his claim that the scandal calls for conversion, and in his call for attention to clericalism. But to see clericalism simply as clergy having power and privilege over lay people misses a crucial piece of the problem. Clericalism can result in 'dysfunctional human formation that fosters narcissism, elitism, entitlement, arrogance, and a lack of true sense of boundaries'.[24] Seminary training that prepares priests to see themselves as superior is clearly problematic. But can we effectively treat clericalism without exposing future priests to gender theory that can help them see how cultural expectations around masculinity prepare them to enact entitlement, take up space, talk over, claim credit, etc.? Recent studies of effective programming suggest that anti-violence education is insufficient. Instead, men need help in identifying their own efforts at performing masculinity as potentially harmful.[25]

Feminist scholar Sarah Ahmed's work on the importance of understanding how gender functions in institutional cultures could also be important for gender cannot be 'undone' only from the ground up. Ahmed's figure of the 'feminist killjoy' suggests the feminist activist's role as truth-teller. For Ahmed, the work of feminism is to see the world differently, to 'venture into secret places of pain, [...] unlearning what we have learnt not to notice'. This is disruptive but, 'We have to do this work if we are to produce critical understandings of how violence, as a relation of force and harm, is directed toward some bodies and not others', and, I might add, performed by some bodies and not others.[26] In the Church, too, resisting violence must involve both personal and communal wrestling with the complexities of masculinity and critical examination of social structures that make women, children, and teens especially vulnerable. We need to find creative ways of disrupting breaking the hold of toxic masculinity in Catholic institutions.

V Conclusion: From the heart of the seminary

I began this essay from the context of the school of theology and ministry that is my new home. Every day I am in the classroom and the chapel, and at table and bar, with current and future priests, sisters, and lay men, and lay women. The stakes seem extraordinarily high – because ministers were and are the abusers and the silence keepers, and because my students care deeply about the Church and this crisis has torn them apart. Like others, we lamented, listened to experts, and offered pastoral expertise. But the most important work has just begun and it will test the limits of our school. In an institutional 'examen,' we are asking ourselves: How have we been complicit with clericalism? How have we challenged it?[27] In open discussion, one on one interviews, as faculty, staff, and students, we are asking these questions. If we are honest, our analysis will take us to questions about gender. As we grapple with the reality of males as the primary perpetrators and enablers of sexual violence, we will have to ask how masculinity is performed at our school, how practices central to our organization, academic programs, social life, and rituals are gendered, how power and powerlessness are experienced and enacted, how masculinity might be 'undone' and reconceived. It will not be easy. It is hard to expose

Julie Hanlon Rubio

the dark underside of things that have long histories, are difficult to see, and may mean a great deal to many in our community. But if the scandal is to be undone, asking the joy-killing questions about masculinity and sexual violence in the Church is unavoidable.

Notes

1. Judith Butler, *Undoing Gender*, New York: Routledge, 2004, pp. 6–7.
2. Judith Butler, 'Performative Acts and Gender Constitution: An Essay in Phenomenology and Feminist Theory', *Theatre Journal*, 40.4 (1988), 519–531.
3. Butler, 'Performative Acts', 526.
4. Judith Butler, *Gender Trouble*, New York: Routledge, 1990, pp. 7–8, 147. See also, Katie Grimes, 'Butler Interprets Aquinas: How to Speak Thomistically about Sex', *Journal of Religious Ethics*, 42.2 (2014), 187–215.
5. Judith Butler is the most influential of contemporary gender theorists, but some question her claim that 'all gender is performance', see Julia Serano, 'Performance Piece', in Kate Bornstein and S. Bear Bergman (eds), *Gender Outlaws: The Next Generation*, Berkeley: Seal Press, 2010, pp. 85–88.
6. See, e.g., Benedict XVI, 'The Church and the Scandal of Sexual Abuse', *Catholic News Agency*, 10 April 2019, https://www.catholicnewsagency.com/news/full-text-of-benedict-xvi-the-church-and-the-scandal-of-sexual-abuse-59639, and Robert Orsi, 'The Study of Religion on the Other Side of Disgust', *Harvard Divinity Bulletin*, 47.1/2 (2019), https://bulletin.hds.harvard.edu/articles/springsummer2019/the-study-of-religion-on-the-other-side-disgust/.
7. Karen J. Terry, *Sexual Offenses and Offenders: Theory, Practice, and Policy, second edition*, Independence: Cengage Learning, 2012.
8. Terry, *Sexual Offenses and Offenders*, pp. 168–72.
9. E.g., through the early 20th century, sex with girls 16 and under was common for adult males. The rights of children to bodily autonomy were only recently established. See Anne Cossins, *Masculinities, Sexualities, and Child Sexual Abuse*, New York: Springer, 2000.
10. Terry, *Sexual Offenses and Offenders*.
11. Cossins, *Masculinities*, p. 91. 90–95% of perpetrators of sexual violence are male.
12. Cossins, *Masculinities*, p. 91.
13. Cossins, *Masculinities*, p. 127.
14. Christine Ricardo and Gary Barker, *Men, Masculinities, Sexual Exploitation, and Sexual Violence: A Literature Review and Call for Action*, 2008, https://promundoglobal.org/wp-content/uploads/2015/01/Men-Masculinities-Sexual-Exploitation-and-Sexual-Violence.pdf.
15. Gerdenio Sonny Manuel, *Living Celibacy: Healthy Pathways for Priests*, Mahwah: Paulist, 2012.
16. Cossins, *Masculinities*, pp. 204–205.
17. Cossins, *Masculinities*, pp. 127–131. See also, Ricardo and Barker, *Men, Masculinities*, 23, 29–32, on the prevalence of same sex abuse by males identifying as heterosexual when access to females is limited (e.g., families, religious institutions, schools, prisons, and the

126

military).

18. Diana Garland, '"Don't Call It an Affair": Understanding and Preventing Clergy Sexual Misconduct with Adults', in Claire M. Renzetti and Sandra Yocum (eds), *Clergy Sexual Abuse: Social Science Perspectives*, Boston: Northeastern University Press, 2013, pp. 118–143.

19. Frederic Martel, *In the Closet of the Vatican: Power, Homosexuality, Hypocrisy*, translated by Shaun Whiteside, London: Bloomsbury, 2019.

20. John Jay College Research Team, *The Causes and Contexts of Sexual Abuse of Minors by Catholic Priests in the United States*, 1950-2010, Washington DC: USCCB, 2011, p. 119. The Charter may be accessed at http://www.usccb.org/issues-and-action/child-and-youth-protection/charter.cfm/.

21. Jennifer Haselberger, speaking at Santa Clara University, Santa Clara, CA, in response to Peter Steinfels, 7 May 2019.

22. Butler, *Undoing Gender*, p. 204.

23. Butler, *Undoing Gender*, pp. 205–206, 216–217.

24. Gerald D. Coleman, 'Seminary Formation in Light of the Sexual Abuse Crisis', in Thomas G. Plante and Kathleen L. McChesney (eds), *Sexual Abuse in the Catholic Church: A Decade in Crisis*, 2002-2012, Santa Barbara, CA: Praeger, 2011, p. 216.

25. Ricardo and Barker, *Men, Masculinities*, pp. 36–38. Efforts to help priests critically reflect on their own gender performance cannot proceed without honesty about sexual orientation. Psychologist T. Plante argues that if 25-40% of priests are gay, while they are no more likely to abuse than other men, because most screeners do not ask about sexual orientation, honest conversations about human formation on sexuality and the subversion of protective in-group behaviours is impossible. Thomas G. Plante, 'Psychological Screening of Clergy Applicants', in Thomas G. Plante and Kathleen L. McChesney (eds), *Sexual Abuse in the Catholic Church: A Decade in Crisis*, 2002-2012, Santa Barbara, CA: Praeger, 2011, pp. 200–201.

26. Sara Ahmed, 'Feminism Hurt/Feminism Hurts', 21 July 2014, https://feministkilljoys.com/2014/07/21/feminist-hurtfeminism-hurts/?fbclid=IwAR2gAa3ktIRWGMop8ap2_zwoIKacaQMDFnASQo4DkT-gzTv-gXRlLcSfO6c.

27. In Ignatian spirituality, the 'examen' is a method of reflecting on daily life with attentiveness to God's presence and direction. Institutional examens invite reflection at a macro-level.

Clerical Masculinities and the Paradigm of Relationality

LEONARDO BOFF

There is a typical clerical masculinity, a consequence of the law of compulsory celibacy for those who serve the community. Ministers' sacred power has been used by some as a way of committing sexual abuses against minors, paedophilia. There is not an adequate education in seminaries for the integration of sexuality without the presence of the feminine. This fact really requires a serious discussion about human sexuality, but this has not yet been initiated by the institutional Church for fear of calling into question the law of celibacy. Celibacy works for a Church whose management is made up exclusively of celibate men and whose structural principle is sacred power and not communion. This sort of Church organisation makes it difficult for celibates to integrate the masculine and feminine dimensions.

It is not possible to talk about masculinity in general terms, since it is flexible and variable according to different cultures and different educational processes that construct specific versions of masculinity.[1]

There is a type of clerical masculinity particular to the Roman Catholic Church as a result of the celibacy law that has come into prominence because of the many crimes of paedophilia perpetrated by clergy. In various statements Pope Francis went straight to the main cause: 'the plague of clericalism, which is the fertile ground for all these disgraces'.[2] In referring to clericalism the Pope seeks to point to the prominence of the celibate clerical state and its abuse of its power. If it were true to itself, it should radiate confidence in and reverence for the sacred. But it was used for the sexual abuse of minors.

Underlying these abuses is the question of sexuality that the official Church refuses to address for fear that the law of celibacy will be called into question. Celibacy is a functional structure for this institution, in a sociological analysis, as a total institution, authoritarian, masculine, patriarchal, hierarchical, which gives no decision-making power to laypeople and excludes women, who are denied full citizenship in the Church. There is no trace of any official Church documents that have ever engaged positively with the work on sexuality done by Sigmund Freud, C. G. Jung, Jacques Lacan, Carl Rogers, Raewyn Connell, Marga J. Ströher, Elizabeth A. Johnson, Donald Winnicott and others.

The institutional Church in general has historically nurtured an attitude of suspicion towards sexuality, one favoured by the dominant patriarchy.[3] It let itself become a prisoner of a prejudiced tradition derived from Platonism and especially from St Augustine. It was Augustine who had the greatest influence on Christian moral teaching, especially as regards sexuality. He regarded sexual activity as the path by which original sin entered the world, with the result that every human being is a sinner without personal sin, but through solidarity with the sin of Adam and Eve. The less sex was for procreation, the more it was *massa damnata*.

Women, by giving birth to sons and daughters, introduce the original evil into the world. Clerical hostility to women draws one of its motivations from here, though it is also influenced by the surrounding patriarchal culture. This interpretation shows the reasons that support the law of celibacy as a theological value, since if a man does not have genital sexual intercourse with a woman, no sons and daughters will be born. This vision is reductionist and concentrates exclusively on the genital sexual dimension.

In all the past and present analyses and condemnations of paedophilia and even of other forms of expressing sexuality, there has been no discussion of the underlying problem, which is precisely that of the role of sexuality itself in human life. Sexuality is much more than genital sexuality. Human beings don't have a sex. We are wholly and entirely sexed in body, soul and spirit; this has to do with the source energy, volcanic energy, I would say, through which by nature and by God's plan live is reproduced on earth.

Paul Ricoeur, who devoted much philosophical reflection to Feud's theory of psychoanalysis, wrote: 'Sexuality, fundamentally, perhaps remains inaccessible to human reflection and inaccessible to human control; and it is perhaps because of this opacity that it is not contained either by the ethics of tenderness or by the non-ethics of eroticism, and also that it cannot even be subsumed into an ethics or a technique.'[4] It lives in between the law of the day, where established rules and behaviour apply, and the law of the night, where drives and spontaneity operate.

Only an approach that combines humanity and spirituality, an ethics of profound respect towards the other sex and self-control over the instinctive force of sex, can turn sexuality into a force for love, fruitful relationships and humanisation.

We are aware of the inadequacy of the education to integrate sexuality into the formation of candidates for the priesthood. They are also part of our type of society, which has still not completely overcome patriarchalism and machismo. In a way they are hostages to this culture. An additional factor is that candidates in seminaries are away from their families, from their mothers and sisters. This produces a sort of atrophy in the construction of identity. There is an excess of Western characteristics of masculinity, rationality, rigidity, the use of force, the desire for power, to take decisions, without the balancing effect of the Western feminine dimension: loving, tender, welcoming, caring, the capacity for dialogue, intuition and spirituality. Clerical masculinity in this way becomes deprived of something essential for complete human development.

The mind sciences have left us in no doubt that a man only matures under the gaze of a woman, and a woman only under the gaze of a man. Man and woman are complete in themselves, but by nature they are relational creatures, they are reciprocal and enrich each other in difference.[5] Why did God create humanity male and female (Gen 1.27)? Not primarily to produce children, but so as not to be alone, to be companions and to be 'one flesh' together (Gen 2.18, 20, 24).

It is worth remembering that there is no absolute sex, but one dominant sex. Genetic analysis shows us that the difference between a man and a woman, in terms of chromosomes, is no more than one chromosome. A woman has two X chromosomes and a man one X and one Y chromosome. From this we can see that the basic sex is female (XX), and the male (XY) is a variation on this.

Sexogenesis has already been in existence for two billion years and has shown that the female comes first in the process of anthropogenesis. The male only came later.[6] This means that in every human being there is 'a second sex'. In every man and every woman there the dimension of the *anima* (feminine) and *animus* (masculine). It is the integration of animus and anima present in each person that produces human and sexual maturity and results in a successful process of individuation.[7]

In the education of future priests and male religious this integration is made more difficult by the absence of one of the dimensions, the feminine. It is replaced by the imagination and fantasies, which, if they are not subjected to discipline and a deep spirituality, can produce substitutes and even perversions, including paedophilia. In this process celibacy is not excluded. It is one of the possible options. But celibacy cannot be the product of a lack of love; on the contrary, it comes from a superabundance of the love of God overflowing to others, especially to those most in need of affection.

To bring about this humanisation of the clergy it would be necessary to abolish the law of obligatory celibacy. But this is what legitimates the exclusive masculine domination of the current structure of the official Church. Only people of the male sex can rise to leadership and organising roles in the community. It would be preferable to have optional celibacy, an option that would be one of a range of charisms and an expression of total dedication to God and the community.

For a long time now theology has been arguing that there is no doctrinal or dogmatic objection to women also being priests, in a style proper to a woman.

Why does the Roman Catholic Church not abolish the law of celibacy? Because it would be in contradiction to its structure. The Church does not have a community style. On the contrary, it is a total, authoritarian, patriarchal and extremely hierarchical institution, a Church structured on the basis of sacred power, concentrated in the hands of a few men, an example of what C.J. Jung condemned: 'where power predominates there is no love or tenderness'. This is what generally occurs, authoritarianism and rigidity in Church structures and in its ministers. Celibacy works for the clerical Church, solely and exclusively. To make good this lack, Pope

Francis never tires of preaching 'tenderness and mercy',[8] and the nature of the Church as communion and synodal and, above all, a Church that goes out to meet people, not bureaucratically, but tenderly and fraternally.

As long as this type of Church exists, we are not likely to see the abolition of the celibacy law. It is useful for the way it designs its structure and the official relationships exclusively among men, the bearers of sacred power, with women excluded. But this dominant model is not pastoral and is not good for the faithful, who look not just for doctrines, but first and foremost for a welcome and introduction to the Christian life. The human being is naturally a knot of relationships facing in all directions. The possibility of relationship is the basic paradigm of our existence and represents, in the view of great cosmologists, the very logic of the universe. Nothing exists outside a relationship. God created humanity male and female (Gen 1.27) so that, being different but not unequal, they could exchange and be together in relationship and communion, joined in friendship and love. This is the ideal type of integrated masculine-feminine sexuality lived by all human beings. Celibacy cannot be an obstacle to this full human development. It cannot be denied to those who serve the community by making it a condition that they live as celibates.

Translated by Francis McDonagh

Notes

1. Arnaud Baubérot, 'One is not born virile, one becomes so', in Alain Corbin, Jean-Jacques Courtine and Georges Vigarello (ed.), *A History of Virility,* New York and Chichester, West Sussex, pp 467-490.
2. Pope Francis, Closing address to the meeting on the protection of minors in the Church, 24 February 2019, 7.2: http://w2.vatican.va/content/francesco/en/speeches/2019/february/documents/papa-francesco_20190224_incontro-protezioneminori-chiusura.html
3. Pierre Bourdieu, Masculine Domination, Cambridge, 2001, pp 85-86; Elizabeth Schüssler-Fiorenza, *But She Said: Feminist Practices of Biblical Interpretation*, Boston, MA, 1992, pp 150-156 (on countering 'malestream theological hermeneutics').
4. Paul Ricœur, 'La Merveille, l'Errance, L'Énigme' Esprit (November 1960), p.1674; *Freud and philosophy. An essay on interpretation*, London and New Haven, CT, 1970.
5. François Héritier, *Masculin-Feminin: La pensée de la différence*, Paris, 1996.
6. Leonardo Boff, 'O processo da sexogênese', in: Leonardo Boff and Rose-Marie Muraro, *Feminino-masculino: Uma nova consciência para o encontro das diferenças*, Rio de Janeiro, 2010, pp 26-29.

7. Larry Richards, *Be a Man!: Becoming the Man God Created You to Be*, New York, 2010.
8. Tenderness and mercy are important themes in Pope Francis' preaching. Many of his talks and homilies stress them. See *Misericordiae Vultus*, the bull establishing the extraordinary Jubilee of Mercy (2015): http://w2.vatican.va/content/francesco/en/bulls/documents/papa-francesco_bolla_20150411_misericordiae-vultus.html; Apostolic Letter *Misericordia et misera* concluding the Jubilee: http://w2.vatican.va/content/francesco/en/apost_letters/documents/papa-francesco-lettera-ap_20161120_misericordia-et-misera.html; Pope Francis, *The Name of God is Mercy*, New York and London, 2016.

Part Five: Theological Forum

The Pan-Amazon Synod

FILIPE MAIA

The Pan-Amazon Synod concluded on October 27, 2019 with a call for a renewed Roman Catholic presence in Amazonia, the recognition of the need for an 'integral ecological conversion', the importance of developing indigenous theologies and inculturated liturgies, and the call for the recognition of women into the permanent diaconate of the Church. This essay details some of the discussion topics addressed by the Synod and locates these conversations in the context of the turbulent Brazilian political scenario, where the Synod has been attacked by political authorities.

It seems appropriate, possibly providential, that just weeks after the fires broke in the Amazon forest in July 2019 bringing the region to international attention, Roman Catholic leaders, environmentalists, and indigenous peoples gathered in the Vatican for the Pan-Amazon Synod. The gathering responds to the urgency that environmental catastrophe poses for life on the planet and places the Church in a prophetic position as a proclaimer of justice in light of the 'cry of the earth and of the poor.'[1]

Pope Francis convoked the Synod in October 2017 and envisioned that it would give the Church a chance to discuss the Amazon region and re-encounter its mission in the area. The three-week long Synod, held in the Vatican in October 2019, welcomed church authorities from nine countries whose territories contain portions of the Amazon forest, in addition to a host of representatives from the more than 390 ethnic groups present in the region. In the Synod's opening mass, Pope Francis called the church to a '*daring prudence*' to 'renew paths of the Church in Amazonia' and closed his homily echoing the words of Brazilian Cardinal Cláudio Hummes, stating that the Amazon territory is holy ground where the memories of missionaries is preserved for their fight on behalf of the forest and its peoples.[2]

The synodal *Instrumentum labouris* adopts the familiar approach of seeing-judging-acting espoused by Latin American liberation theologians. The document opens with a chapter on 'The Voice of the Amazon', moves to an eco-theological session calling for an 'Integral Ecology', and concludes with a call to action, 'A Prophetic Church in the Amazon'. The Synod minces no words when it demands an 'integral ecological conversion' from the Church (*Instrumentum labouris* 5). Data included in the document shows that nothing short of a conversion could properly address the situation in the Amazon region. Experts place Amazonia as the second most vulnerable habitat in the planet, next only to the Arctic. A 4°C increase in temperature and/or a 40% level of deforestation can lead to points of no return toward desertification. In 2018, leading Brazilian climate scientist, Carlos Nobre, and renowned biologist Thomas Lovejoy argued that desertification in the Amazon could be expected to begin when deforestation reaches 20-25% of the Amazon area.[3] After the fires and the extravagant increase of deforestation rates in August 2019, Nobre fears a tipping point is dangerously close.[4]

Needless to say, the effects of this would be devastating, environmentally *and* socially. The Synod ably connects data on deforestation with the social reality of Amazonia: the criminalization and assassination of indigenous leaders, lack of public policies for land demarcation, appropriation and privatization of natural goods, destruction of the forest for large 'development' projects, pollution, alcoholism, human trafficking, etc. These are symptoms of what Pope Francis addressed as 'disconnection' and 'indifference' to the cries of the earth and of the poor (*Laudato Si'* 49, 91). For Francis, the ecological crisis demands an integral approach.

The Synod acknowledges that this holistic attitude will be met with resistance from '[economic] interests and a technocratic paradigm [that] rebuff[s] any attempt to change' (*Instrumentum labouris* 41). These interests are indeed paramount in Amazonia. In light of lowering oil prices, Venezuela adopted an aggressive policy to incentivize mining in the Amazon region, which included the concession of lands to Chinese mining companies. Bolivia, Paraguay, and Peru continue to wrestle with criminal fires in its Amazon regions and the influence of groups that seek to clear the forest for farming and cattle raising, a criminal activity that often goes unchallenged by government officials. President Evo Morales of Bolivia, for example, was pressured to suspend a law that authorizes 'controlled fires' in Amazonia. In all these cases, the 'technocratic paradigm' and the need to 'develop' the region continue to be the driving force justifying the destruction of forest areas.

Brazil, a country whose territory embraces more than 60% of the Amazon forest, is currently a key site of the anti-environmentalist agenda. Guided by its newly elected, far-right President, Jair Bolsonaro, Brazilian political authorities have carefully scrutinized the Pan-Amazon Synod. Elected for office in October 2018, Bolsonaro ran a campaign that promised not a 'single additional millimetre' of land demarcations for indigenous peoples and loose environmental regulations, all the while publicly endorsing agrobusiness mammoths that eye the Amazon as a site for massive profit-making. Bolsonaro's cabinet secretary for institutional security, General Augusto Heleno, portrayed the Synod as a 'leftist' threat to national security and warned against international interference in Brazilian domestic policies.[5] Reports indicate that the government spied on Brazilian Bishops and others involved with the planning of the Synod.[6]

Internationally, ultraconservative Catholic groups voice criticism of what they perceive as 'neopagan' religious ideas stated in the Instrumentum labouris for the Amazon Synod. One such report indicts the document of espousing 'syncretism' and, worse still, 'apostasy or false religion'.[7] Such critics possibly eye the important positions assumed by the Synod with respect to the importance of an Amazonian indigenous theology, which shall incorporate the 'original myths, traditions, symbols, knowledge, rites and celebrations that include transcendent, community and ecological dimensions' (Instrumentum labouris 98). The synodal final document insists on the importance of inculturation, both theological and liturgical, and it offers some practical recommendations in that regard.

Another topic addressed by synodal documents that gained significant attention is the call to integrate social and ecological concerns with women's struggles. The Synod's final document includes a request for the ordination of women to the permanent diaconate while acknowledging the crucial role women continue to play in the struggle for the environment in Amazonia.[8] This is far from good news for women who have sought recognition for their ministries in the Roman Catholic Church, but it is certainly a promising outcome of the Synod's deliberations. The ability to connect pastoral needs in Amazonia, the leadership of women, and environmental justice is perhaps the greatest blow of fresh air the Synod offers to the Church.

Liberation theologian Leonardo Boff, who writes extensively on theology and the environment, portrayed the Synod as ushering in a 'new type of presence of the Church in the Americas' and a new 'degree of consciousness' about the importance of Amazonia for the Earth's climate and for the future of life in the planet.[9] Boff perceives the Synod as the fruitful result of Pope Francis' courageous leadership, perhaps best exemplified by his 2015-speech in Bolivia, where he famously asked for forgiveness 'not only for the offenses of the Church, but also for the crimes committed against indigenous peoples during the so-called conquest of the Americas'.[10] As Boff suggests, these statements are materialized in the efforts of the Pan-Amazon Synod.

And they might be symbolized by an auspicious moment at the conclusion of the Synod. On October 20, a group of Bishops and participants gathered at the Catacombs of Domitila in Rome and affirmed their commitment to listening to the cry of the earth and of the poor. The event is reminiscent of a similar gathering at the concluding session of Vatican II where Bishops, led by Archbishop Hélder Cámara, firmed the 'Pact of the Catacombs' and swore to commit their lives and ministries to the poor, a commitment known to have helped the birth of liberation theologies. The pact firmed in the gathering of 2019, 'Pact of the Catacombs for the Common Home', might be our hope for the dawning of a new prophetic era for the Church. This may be our hope for a fresh wind of the Spirit, blowing from the crevices of the Amazon.

Notes

1. The expression was first proposed by Leonardo Boff, *Cry of the Earth, Cry of the Poor*, Maryknoll: Orbis Books, 1997, and is repeated in Pope Francis's *Laudato Si'*.
2. Pope Francis, 'Homily of Pope Francis, Holy Mass for the opening of the Synod of Bishops for the Pan-Amazon Region', 6 October 2019, http://w2.vatican.va/content/

francesco/en/homilies/2019/documents/papa-francesco_20191006_omelia-sinodo-amazzonia.html.

3. Thomas E. Lovejoy and Carlos Nobre, 'Amazon Tipping Point', *Science Advances*, 4.2 (2018): eaat2340, doi: 10.1126/sciadv.aat2340.

4. Dom Phillips, 'Amazon Rainforest "Close to Irreversible Tipping Point"', *The Guardian*, 23 October 2019, http://www.theguardian.com/environment/2019/oct/23/amazon-rainforest-close-to-irreversible-tipping-point.

5. Eduardo Campos Lima, 'Eyeing Amazon Synod, Brazil Accuses Church of "Leftist Agenda"', *National Catholic Reporter*, 26 February 2019, https://www.ncronline.org/news/environment/eyeing-amazon-synod-brazil-accuses-church-leftist-agenda.

6. Tânia Monteiro, 'Planalto vê Igreja Católica como potencial opositora', O Estado de São Paulo, 10 February 2019, https://politica.estadao.com.br/noticias/geral,planalto-ve-igreja-catolica-como-potencial-opositora,70002714758.

7. Charles Pope, 'Don't Be Tempted by False Gardens – We Preach Christ Crucified', *Pan-Amazon Synod Watch* (blog), 18 October 2019, https://panamazonsynodwatch.info/feature/dont-be-tempted-by-false-gardens-we-preach-christ-crucified/.

8. See Vatican News, 'Amazon Synod: The Church Committed to Be an Ally with Amazonia', *Vatican News*, 26 October 2019, https://www.vaticannews.va/en/vatican-city/news/2019-10/amazon-synod-final-document.html; Christopher Lamb, 'Amazon Synod: Bishops to Vote on Women Deacons', *The Tablet: The International Catholic News Weekly*, 22 October 2019, https://www.thetablet.co.uk/news/12146/amazon-synod-bishops-to-vote-on-women-deacons.

9. Leonardo Boff, 'Como o Sínodo Panamazônico pode nos surpreender', *Leonardo Boff* (blog), 7 October 2019, https://leonardoboff.wordpress.com/2019/10/06/como-o-sinodo-panamazonico-pode-nos-surpreender/.

10. Pablo Ordaz, 'El Papa pide perdón por los crímenes durante la conquista de América', *El País*, 10 July 2015, https://elpais.com/internacional/2015/07/10/actualidad/1436484652_422140.html.

The Vatican, China, and the Future of the Chinese Catholic Church

BENOÎT VERMANDER SJ

In September 2018, the Holy See signed a provisional agreement with the Chinese government relating to the process of the appointment of bishops. This contribution locates that agreement in its historical context, evaluates its application just over a year after its signing, and sketches out some angles. It sheds light on the positive and necessary character of the agreement while emphasising that it operates within the context of a hardening of China's religious policies. Dialogue and trust have been re-established, but the way forward remains narrow and risky.

I Introduction

On 22 September 2018 the Vatican announced that it had signed a 'Provisional Agreement' with the Chinese government relating to a joint mechanism for the appointment of future bishops, a mechanism whose precise content has not been revealed. It was accompanied by a decision by Pope Francis to readmit bishops ordained without pontifical mandate to fully communion.[1] Although very brief, this article aims to locate the Agreement in its context, evaluate its effects, and draw out its significance for the universal Church.

II China and the Vatican: Context

Following the 1911 Revolution, the Chinese Republic sought to promote the development of 'national' and modern' religions, in place of 'superstitions'. From 1912 national religious associations were founded,[2] before being re-founded in line with the needs of the new regime from 1949. The state thus ensures its control – although not without considerable resistance – over religious organisations and activities as it does over other expressions of civil society. After the turbulence of the cultural revolution (1966-1976) the institutional framework governing relationships between the state and religion was reaffirmed on the foundations constructed in the immediate aftermath of 1949. Article 36 of the Constitution defines the rights and duties of religions in the People's Republic of China. 'Citizens of the People's Republic of China enjoy freedom of religious belief. No state organ, public organisation, or individual may compel citizens to believe in, or not to believe in, any religion; nor may they discriminate against citizens who believe in, or do not believe in, any religion.' The constitutional provisions cited above are completed by the 'Provisions relating to religious affairs' which took effect in March 2005 and were profoundly refashioned in a very restricted way in 2017-2018.[3] Furthermore, since 2013 the development of a renewed form of 'civil religion' frames religion much more narrowly. All religions are required to further 'sinicise' themselves which in practice requires that they adopt uncritically the orthodoxy promoted by the Party.[4]

Institutional and political considerations are not enough to gauge the situation of the Church within Chinese society. A 'Catholicism of the fields' had developed in China, which firmly maintained its own traditions until the massive migration to the cities in the first decade of the twenty-first century. It is already apparent that this movement has profoundly shaken the traditional structure of Chinese Catholicism.

The official Church has some 1900 priests, while the clandestine Church has around 1200. Several estimates mention a total Catholic faithful of between 10 and 12 million.[5] Anthony Lam of the Holy Spirit Centre in Hong Kong has studied the public data and correlated them with his local interviews. His conclusion is that the number of Catholics in China peaked at 12 million in 2005, then plateaued for several years, and is now in decline. Furthermore, still according to Lam's estimates, between 1996 and 2014 the number of male vocations dropped from 2300 to 1260, while female vocations collapsed from 2500 to 156. The number of ordinations went from 134 in 2000 to 78 in 2014.

III From Benedict XVI's Letter to Francis' Letter

Following the creation of the Catholic Patriotic Association in 1957, followed by the ordinations of official bishops (ordinations which were canonically valid but held without the approval of the Pope) 'special faculties' were granted to the bishops who had remained in communion with Rome in order to permit them to ordain new bishops in an autonomous way in case of need. On 30 June 2007, the Vatican made public a letter from Benedict XVI to 'the clergy and faithful of the Catholic Church in China', which revoked these special faculties, justifying this change of course because 'the solution to existing problems cannot be pursued via an ongoing conflict with the legitimate civil authorities.'

Following the election of Pope Francis,[6] the Chinese authorities listened to the invitation and negotiations began again, which led to the agreement mentioned above in September 2018. The fact that the agreement does not specify the precise mechanism for the appointment of bishops had led to much ink being spilled, although the question is in fact secondary: whether the names of *episcopabili* are initially proposed by the Vatican or the government is of little importance since on the one hand both parties maintain the power of veto, and on the other, in practice there are few serious candidates for each See. In any case, both parties have decided to review the mechanism for appointment in view of experience accumulated over the next two or three years.

Another debate concerned the point that while the Vatican had accepted the reintegration of the eight official bishops who had not until now been canonically recognised, but nothing had been said publicly about the fate of the twenty or so bishops who are not recognised by the government. The question remains somewhat clouded, but seems to be being dealt with in a pragmatic manner. In a great many cases it seems that it will be resolved at the point of their succession, when compromise candidates will be appointed.

In his *Message to the Catholics of China and to the universal Church* (26 September 2018), Francis forcefully expresses the ultimate aims of the Agreement:

'I now turn with respect to the leaders of the People's Republic of China and renew my invitation to continue, with trust, courage and far-sightedness, the dialogue begun some time ago … In this way, China and the Apostolic See, called by history to an arduous yet exciting task, will be able to act more positively for the orderly and harmonious growth of the Catholic community in China. They will make efforts to promote the integral development of society by ensuring greater respect for the human person, also in the religious sphere, and will work concretely to protect the environment in which we live and to build a future of peace and fraternity between peoples.'

IV Following the agreement

The new mechanism has already resulted in the ordination of two new bishops: Mgr Antoine Yao Shun, for the diocese of Jining, in Inner Mongolia, on 26 August 2019, and Mgr Stephen Xu Hongwei, appointed coadjutor bishop of the diocese of Hanzhong, in Shannxi province, two days later. The Holy See confirmed that these two ordinations took place in the context of the Agreement, even though the Pope had already appointed Mgr Yao and Mgr Xu prior to its signing.[8] Sources of tensions nonetheless subsist, some coming from the local and governmental authorities, others internal to the Chinese Church, and others fomented by an international 'anti-Francis' movement.[9]

The Agreement might well allow the Church to rebuild its internal unity. But one cannot exclude the possibility of a growing hiatus between progress at the diplomatic level and ideological pressures exerted on religious organisations which, at a certain level, will inevitably provoke new conflicts.

Finally, we should note two further points. First, even though it takes place under strict political control, the appointment process for Chinese bishops today includes representatives of the priests, Religious, and faithful of the dioceses, with the approval of the Holy See; if this continues for some time, it could have repercussions in other ecclesial contexts. Second, in his *Message*, Francis was careful not to stay at the purely ecclesial level: he emphasised the importance of China becoming part of questions of global governance, and asked the universal Church to better appreciate and accept the best of the spiritual treasures of Chinese Catholicism. These two points can contribute to the invigoration the interior spirit of Chinese Christian communities, beyond political twists and turns.

Translated by Patricia Kelly

Notes

1. Missions etrangères de Paris, 'Accord Chine-Vatican: "Pour la première fois, tous les évêques de Chine sont en communion avec Rome"', 24 September 2019, https:// missionsetrangeres.com/eglises-asie/2018-09-24-accord-chine-vatican-pour-la-premiere-fois-tous-les-eveques-de-chine-sont-en-communion-avec-rome/.
2. Cf. Vincent Goossaert, 'Republican Church Engineering: The National Religious Associations in 1912 China', in Mayfair Mei-hui Yang (ed.), *Chinese Religiosities, Afflictions of Modernity and State Formation*, Berkeley: University of California Press, 2008, pp. 209–232.
3. For an English translation of the new provisions, see http://www.chinalawtranslate.com/宗教事务条例-2017/?lang=en.
4. See Benoît Vermander, 'Le rêve chinois de religion civile', Esprit, no. 451 (Jan-Feb 2019), 171–182; Benoît Vermander, 'Sinicizing Religions, Sinicizing Religious Studies', *Religions*, 10/137 (2019), 10 (137), 1–23, doi: 10.3390/rel10020137.
5. Ian Johnson, 'How the Top-heavy Catholic Church Is Losing the Ground Game in China', *America Magazine*, 18 September 2017.
6. On the reasons why the Chinese authorities showed more openness to Francis than to Benedict XVI, , see Federico Lombardi, 'Verso una Chiesa pienamente cinese e pienamente cattolica. La via tracciata da Benedetto XVI e Francesco', *La Civiltà Cattolica*, no. 4017 (2017), 209–220.
7. Francis, 'Message of the Holy Father to the Catholics of China and to the universal Church', http://w2.vatican.va/content/francesco/en/messages/pont-messages/2018/documents/papa-francesco_20180926_messaggio-cattolici-cinesi.html #10.
8. Missions etrangères de Paris, 'Deux évêques chinois ordonnés pour la première fois depuis la signature de l'accord sino-vatican', 29 August 2019, https://missionsetrangeres.com/eglises-asie/deux-eveques-chinois-ordonnes-pour-la-premiere-fois-depuis-la-signature-de-laccord-sino-vatican/.
9. We see an example of a negative evaluation of the Agreement and its consequences in Bernardo Cervellera, 'Religious Policy in China before and after the Sino-Vatican agreement', *Asia News*, 12 September 2019. The documents he cites about the discussions held by the Chinese authorities on their religious policies as a whole are pertinent. At the same time the directions promoted by Francis, albeit clearly announced by him, are not at all taken into account, and no strategy other than full-on confrontation is even envisaged. The denial of the real situation of contemporary Chinese society, and with nostalgia for a model of the Church which is disappearing (and idealist), are expressed here without nuance.

Contributors

RAEWYN CONNELL is Professor Emerita at the University of Sydney, Life Member of the National Tertiary Education Union, and one of Australia's leading social scientists. She helped establish the field of research on masculinities, and has also worked in education, history, social theory and studies of knowledge. For details see www.raewynconnell.net.

Address: Mrs R. Connell, 342 Annandale Street, Annandale, NSW 2038 Australia

Email: raewyn.connell@gmail.com

HERBERT ANDERSON is a Lutheran Pastor and Professor Emeritus of Pastoral Theology from Catholic Theological Union in Chicago. He is the author or co-author of several books and numerous articles on a wide range of topics from men's grief to the wisdom of Dr. Seuss. His most recent book, written with Karen Speerstra, is *The Divine Art of Dying: How to Live Well While Dying*. After 50 years of teaching pastoral care in theological seminaries, he is retired and lives among the vineyards in Sonoma, California.

Address: Herbert Anderson, 19495 Laurelbrook Ct, Sonoma, CA 95476 USA

Email: herbert.e.anderson@icloud.com

MANUEL VILLALOBOS MENDOZA is an Affiliated Assistant Professor of New Testament Interpretation at Chicago Theological Seminary. He is the author of *Abject Bodies in the Gospel of Mark* (2012); *When Men Were Not Men: Masculinity and Otherness in the Pastoral Epistles* (2014), and *Masculinidad y Otredad en Crisis en las Epístolas Pastorales* (2019).

Address: Manuel Villalobos Mendoza, 5540 S. Everett, Chicago, Il, 60637, USA

Email: villa67lobos@gmail.com

EZRA CHITANDO is Professor of History and Phenomenology of Religion in the Department of Religious Studies, Classics and Philosophy at the University of Zimbabwe, and Theology Consultant on HIV and AIDS for the World Council of Churches (WCC) Ecumenical HIV and AIDS Initiatives and Advocacy (EHAIA). His research, publication and activist interest include, religion and: gender, masculinities, HIV, human security, development, climate change and politics.

Address: Prof. Ezra Chitando, World Council of Churches. c/o Dominican Convent, P. B. CH 7408, Chisipite, Harare, Zimbabwe

Email: chitsa21@yahoo.com

VINCENT LLOYD is Associate Professor of Theology and Religious Studies at Villanova University. He co-edits the journal *Political Theology* and directs the Villanova Political Theology Project. Lloyd is the author of *Break Every Yoke: Religion, Justice, and the Abolition of Prisons*, with Joshua Dubler (2019); *In Defense of Charisma* (2018); and *Black Natural Law* (2016). He also co-edited *Anti-Blackness and Christian Ethics* (2017), with Andrew Prevot.

Address: Vincent Lloyd, Department of Theology and Religious Studies, 800 E. Lancaster Ave., Villanova, PA 19085, USA

Email: vincent.lloyd@villanova.edu

NICHOLAS DENYSENKO serves as Emil and Elfriede Jochum Professor and Chair at Valparaiso University. He previously taught at Loyola Marymount University in Los Angeles (2010–2017). His most recent books are *The People's Faith: The Liturgy of the Faithful in Orthodoxy* (2018), and *The Orthodox Church in Ukraine: A Century of Separation* (2018). He is a deacon of the Orthodox Church in America, ordained in 2003.

Address: Nicholas Denysenko, Valparaiso University, 1400 Chapel Drive, ASB 306, Valparaiso, IN 46383

Email: nicholas.denysenko@valpo.edu

SHYAM PAKHARE is Assistant Professor of History at K.C. College, affiliated with the University of Mumbai. His area of research is Gandhi, India's struggle for freedom and masculinities.

Address: Prof. Dr. Shyam Pakhare, Department of History, 124, Dinshaw Wachha Road, Churchgate, Mumbai 20
Email: shyam.pakhare111@gmail.com

ANGÉLICA OTAZÚ, DPhil, in the area of Catholic Theology through the Free University of Berlin, Degree in Pastoral Science and Philosophy. Professor of Catechetical Pastoral and Ethics at the Catholic University 'Nuestra Señora de la Asunción' (Asunción, Paraguay). Some of her publications include: *Práctica y Semántica en la Evangelización de los Guaraníes del Paraguay* (S. XVI–XVIII) (2006); 'La influencia de la lengua guaraní a nivel local y regional', Estudios Paraguayos 2 (2018).

Address: Prof. Dr. Angelica Otazú, Luis A. Alberto de Herrera 905, Asunción – Paraguay
Email: potykuru@hotmail.com

THERESIA HEIMERL studied German and Classical Philology and Catholic theology in Graz and Würzburg from 2003 onwards. She is currently professor of religious studies at the theological faculty in Graz. The main areas of her work are the study of religion in Europe, body-gender-religion, and religion and film and TV

Address: Prof. Dr. Theresia Heimerl, Institut für Religionswissenschaft, Heinrichstrasse 78, A-8010 Graz, Austria
Email: theresia.heimerl@uni-graz.at

JULIE HANLON RUBIO joined the faculty at Jesuit School of Theology of Santa Clara University in Berkeley, California, after 19 years at St. Louis University. She writes about Catholic social thought as it relates to sex, gender, marriage, and family. She is the author of four books, including *Hope for Common Ground: Mediating the Personal and the Political in a Divided Church* (2016), which won the College Theology Society's annual book award. Currently, she is writing a book called Catholic and Feminist: Is It Still Possible?

Address: Prof. Dr. Julie Hanlon Rubio, Jesuit School of Theology of

Santa Clara, 1735 Leroy Ave., Berkeley, CA 94709, USA
  Email: jmkrubio@gmail.com

LEONARDO BOFF, born 1938, is a theologian, philosopher and writer. He was professor of theology at the Franciscan Institute in Petrópolis for 22 years and then professor of ethics and the philosophy of religion at the state university of Rio de Janeiro, as well as visiting professor at various universities. He publishes in the areas of theology, philosophy, ethics and ecology. He lives in Petrópolis, Rio de Janeiro, Brazil.

  Address: Estrada do Mombaça, 1800, Bairro Jardim Araras, 25725-290 Petrópolis, RJ, Brazil.
  Email: Lboff@leonardoboff.eco.br

FILIPE MAIA is Assistant Professor of Theology at Boston University School of Theology. His research focuses on liberation theologies and philosophies, theology and economics, and the Christian eschatological imagination. He is currently completing a book that offers an analysis of the debate in critical theory addressing the 'financialization' of capitalism to show how future-talk is ubiquitous to financial discourse and how contemporary finance engenders a particular mode of temporality.

  Address: Dr. Filipe Maia, Boston University School of Theology, 745 Commonwealth Avenue, mailbox 250, Boston, MA 02215, USA
  Email: fmaia@bu.edu

BENOÎT VERMANDER, S.J. is Professor of Religious Studies in the Faculty of Philosophy at Fudan University, Shanghai. His recent publications include *Shanghai Sacred: The Religious Landscape of a Global City* (with Liz Hingley and Liang Zhang, 2018); *Versailles, la République et la Nation* (2018); and *Corporate Social Responsibility in China* (2014).

  Address: Prof. Benoît Vermander, School of Philosophy, Fudan University, 220 Handan Road, Shanghai 200433 , P.R.China
  Email: benoit.vermander@gmail.com

CONCILIUM
International Journal of Theology

FOUNDERS
Anton van den Boogaard; Paul Brand; Yves Congar, OP; Hans Küng;
Johann Baptist Metz; Karl Rahner, SJ; Edward Schillebeeckx

BOARD OF DIRECTORS
President: Thierry-Marie Courau OP
Vice-Presidents: Linda Hogan and Daniel Franklin Pilario CM

BOARD OF EDITORS
Susan Abraham, Los Angeles (USA)
Michel Andraos, Chicago (USA)
Mile Babic´ OFM, Sarajevo (Bosna i Hercegovina)
Antony John Baptist, Bangalore (India)
Michelle Becka, Würzburg (Deutschland)
Bernadeth Caero Bustillos, Osnabrück (Deutschland)
Catherine Cornille, Boston (USA)
Thierry-Marie Courau OP, Paris (France)
Geraldo Luiz De Mori SJ, Belo Horizonte (Brasil)
Enrico Galavotti, Chieti (Italia)
Margareta Gruber OSF, Vallendar (Deutschland)
Linda Hogan, Dublin (Ireland)
Huang Po-Ho, Tainan (Zhōnghuá Mínguó)
Stefanie Knauss, Villanova (USA)
Carlos Mendoza-Álvarez OP, Ciudad de México (México)
Gianluca Montaldi FN, Brescia (Italia)
Agbonkhianmeghe Orobator SJ, Nairobi (Kenya)
Daniel Franklin Pilario CM, Quezon City (Filipinas)
Léonard Santedi Kinkupu, Kinshasa (RD Congo)
João J. Vila-Chã SJ, Roma (Italia)

PUBLISHERS
SCM Press (London, UK)
Matthias-Grünewald Verlag (Ostfildern, Germany)
Editrice Queriniana (Brescia, Italy)
Editorial Verbo Divino (Estella, Spain)
EditoraVozes (Petropolis, Brazil)

Concilium Secretariat:
Couvent de l'Annonciation
222 rue du Faubourg Saint-Honoré
75008 – Paris (France)
secretariat.concilium@gmail.com
Executive secretary: Gianluca Montaldi FN

http://www.concilium.in

Concilium Subscription Information

July	**2020/3:** *Theology, Power and Governance*
October	**2020/4:** *Signs of Hope for Muslim-Christian Dialogue*
December	**2020/5:** *Differently Able: for a Church Where All Belong*
February	**2021/1:** *Church in the Borders*
April	**2021/2:** *Synodality*

New subscribers: to receive the next five issues of Concilium please copy this form, complete it in block capitals and send it with your payment to the address below. Alternatively subscribe online at www.conciliumjournal.co.uk

Please enter my annual subscription for Concilium starting with issue 2020/3.

Individuals
_____ £52 UK
_____ £75 overseas and (Euro €92, US $110)

Institutions
_____ £75 UK
_____ £95 overseas and (Euro €120, US $145)

Postage included – airmail for overseas subscribers

Payment Details:
Payment can be made by cheque (£ Sterling only), by credit/debit card or bank transfer.
a. I enclose a cheque for £ _____ Payable to Hymns Ancient and Modern Ltd
b. To pay by Visa/Mastercard please contact us on +44(0)1603 785911 or go to www.conciliumjournal.co.uk
c. To pay in US $ or Euro € by bank transfer please contact us on +44(0)1603 785911

Contact Details:
Name ....
Address ....
....
Telephone .... E-mail ....

Send your order to *Concilium*, **Hymns Ancient and Modern Ltd**
13a Hellesdon Park Road, Norwich NR6 5DR, UK
E-mail: concilium@hymnsam.co.uk
or order online at www.conciliumjournal.co.uk

Customer service information
All orders must be prepaid. Your subscription will begin with the next issue of Concilium. If you have any queries or require Information about other payment methods, please contact our Customer Services department.